# OUR VETERANS
# NEED YOUR HELP!

## AMERICA'S VETERANS...

- Represent our DIVERSITY and STRENGTH
- VOLUNTEER to defend our freedoms
- Make tremendous SACRIFICES on our behalf
- Continue to SERVE and LEAD when they return home
- DESERVE our thanks - and have EARNED our support!

See reverse to learn more!

## Our truck is coming
## to your street:

**Pick-Up Date**

Thursday, November 17

**UNITED WAR
VETERANS
RECYCLING.**

## Donate your usable
## clothing and goods...
## We'll pick them up!

Visit uwvcpickup.org or call 1.888.821.UWVC (8982)

13-9295***********************ECRWSS**R002
013-10251-1117
RESIDENT
1964 RIVER RD UNIT 29
CALVERTON, NY 11933-1616

# Afrocentric
# Sermons

# Afrocentric Sermons

## The Beauty of Blackness in the Bible

Kenneth L. Waters, Sr.

Judson Press ® Valley Forge

Afrocentric Sermons: The Beauty of Blackness in the Bible

© 1993
Judson Press, Valley Forge, PA 19482-0851

**Library of Congress Cataloging-in-Publication Data**

Waters, Kenneth L., 1953–
    Afrocentric sermons : the beauty of blackness in the Bible / by
Kenneth L. Waters, Sr.
        p.   cm.
    Includes bibliographical references and index.
    ISBN 0-8170-1199-4
    1. Afro-Americans—Religion.  2. Blacks in the Bible—Sermons.
3. Sermons, American–Afro-American authors.   I. Title.
BR563.N4W35   1993
252'.0089'96–dc20                                        93-34347

Printed in the U.S.A.
7 6 5 4 3
10 09 08 07 06 05 04 03 02 01 00 99 98

To Ollie James Waters and Marie Porter Waters
of El Paso, Texas, my father and mother,
who taught me Christian faith
and who instilled within me
self-respect and a sense
of racial pride

# Contents

# Foreword

W ITHOUT QUESTION, preaching in the black church often expresses itself as a "folk and fine art." The colorful
images, the rich cadences of rhetorical flourishes, the dramatic
reenlivening of the ancient biblical stories, and not infrequently the
call to prophetic action contribute to the sermon being the center-
piece of the worship experience among African Americans. Other
racial and ethnic groups have tended to focus on the aesthetics of
the sanctuary or the liturgy as a whole or even on the music, while
for some reason the preached word tends to be short and woefully
inconsequential. No doubt, the same may be said of a number of
black congregations within so-called mainstream American Prot-
estantism. Not so certainly for Kenneth L. Waters, Sr., who, while
being a pastor of a black congregation within a mainline Prot-
estant denomination, knows full well the historic importance of
the sermon within the context of African American life and culture — the sermon as a key to exhortation, teaching, persuasion,
and challenge.

Drawing upon years of studying aspects of ancient black history prior to the relatively modern African slave trade, Waters has
had enough of the kind of "learned" preaching that establishes
itself only through an exclusive Eurocentric view of history and
culture. Instead of limiting black history to a period that dates
back merely to the slave trade, he seeks to enlighten readers of
all racial and ethnic groups about those instructive ways that the

Bible serves as an ancient compendium of black history. With the publication of this refreshing collection of Afrocentric sermons, the author makes available to a much wider audience of Christian readers themes, historical details, and timely issues that heretofore were available only to his own congregation in Los Angeles or to other local groups that have heard him preach and lecture. While other black pastors have certainly taken similar approaches to some of their preaching assignments, I know of no other minister who has done so in as systematic and well-documented a manner as Kenneth Waters.

Clearly, *Afrocentric Sermons* is an idea whose time not only has come, but whose time has been long overdue! It is our good fortune to be part of the closing decade of the present century and to see within our lifetime the blossoming of multiculturalism and Afrocentrism — both of which are multidimensional and represent a range of different viewpoints. Nevertheless, this is a decade of challenge and change with both multiculturalism and Afrocentrism inviting all of us to reexamine carefully the traditional narrow parameters of Eurocentric thought and community practice. Although it is seldom admitted, the dominance of Eurocentrism, through which all things European in origin are valued most and things African are valued least, has done untold harm, often quite subtly, to the confidence and self-esteem of people of color, especially African Americans. The provocative sermons collected here have helped and will help African Americans not only better cope with some of the historical damage done to them by the unfortunate biases and curricular contrivances of the white brothers and sisters, but it will also enable them to see the Bible in a new light as truly a liberating and inclusive witness!

That our decade is one of great challenge and change is certified by the publication of a whole new genre of Afrocentric biblical scholarship generated by an increasing number of black Bible scholars who could no longer wait for others to include their history as part of the ancient biblical narratives. Kenneth Waters has become a pastoral colleague with this new generation of black biblical scholars. In the ten captivating sermons in this book, he alerts us to the great new possibilities for empowerment that result when the resources of black biblical scholarship are brought to bear on the weekly task of preaching the Word to local congregations who daily struggle for greater meaning and coherence in their lives within a society that more often than not seems to be at war with them.

In 1926, the son of a Methodist preacher in Harlem, Countee Cullen, published an anthology of poems typical of the Harlem Renaissance. The book was entitled *Copper Sun,* and the first poem in it, "From the Dark Tower," displayed a deep understanding of the black American experience of unmerited suffering. Somehow, as I read and reread the pages of this book by Kenneth Waters, my mind kept traveling back to ideas expressed in this poem. Cullen declared that African Americans would not always "plant while others reap" while remaining "abject and mute," and asserted that we African American sisters and brothers were "not made eternally to weep." For much too long in America — this land that at times seems alien to our noblest aspirations — we have been "abject and mute." I refer not to the complacent and privileged "Buppies" within our ranks; rather, I think of the faces of our urban and rural poor, the throngs of incarcerated black men and women, and the masses of forgotten America who need a fresh word of hope and love. I am grateful that Kenneth Waters has not forgotten their plight and their continuing tears, but instead has taken the time to craft for us and for them a renewed word from the Lord that can turn their tears into laughter and utter joy.

CAIN HOPE FELDER, PH.D
Professor, New Testament Language and Literature
Howard University, School of Divinity
Washington, D.C.

# Acknowledgments

I WISH TO ACKNOWLEDGE with deep appreciation Dr. Cain Hope Felder, Professor of New Testament Language and Literature at the Divinity School of Howard University, who wrote the foreword for this book and whose recommendations for the improvement of this manuscript were of immense value. Any shortfall remaining in these pages is certainly mine alone.

I wish also to acknowledge several people who were formative influences upon my thought: Dr. Zan W. Holmes, Jr., Associate Professor of Preaching at the Perkins School of Theology and Senior Pastor of the St. Luke "Community" United Methodist Church, who was the first person I ever heard speak of racism as it manifests itself in the English language and media, when he was featured speaker for the North Texas Annual Conference of the United Methodist Church in the mid-1980s; Dr. Cornelius Henderson, President-Dean of the Gammon Theological Seminary in Atlanta, whose Afrocentric preaching on the few occasions that I have heard him left an indelible mark upon me; the Right Reverend John Hurst Adams, Presiding Bishop of the Seventh Episcopal District of the African Methodist Episcopal Church, at whose hands I was ordained and whose prophetic courage and passion for justice remain an inspiration to me; Dr. Dolly Deselle Adams, Supervisor of Missions and Women's Work for the Seventh District, a leader who has always elicited my admiration; Dr. William R. Farmer, Professor of New Testament Language and Literature at Perkins School of Theology, my academic mentor, who introduced me to the works of Professor F. M. Snowden, Jr., and Howard Thurman when I was a Ph.D. candidate in New Testament at Southern Methodist University; the Right Reverend Henry Wendell Murph, retired Presiding Bishop of the Fifth Episcopal District of the African Methodist Episcopal Church, a good friend who encouraged me through critical periods in my life and ministry; Geraldine Murph, whose kindness and warmness I will always remember; the Reverend Robert Smith, Superintendent of the Los Angeles District of the United Methodist Church, who has also been a pastor, a friend, and a counselor to me and has stood with me in the storm; Gwendolyn Smith, who has been a source of encouragement to me; the Reverend Albert Smith, retired Pastor of the First United Baptist Church of El Paso, Texas, my "father in the ministry," who recognized my call to the gospel ministry when I was a teenager; Esther Smith, who was an example of strength and spirituality to me during my growing years. None of these people is responsible for the shape and content of these messages, nor is it suggested that any one of them would agree with all that I have said. Still they are people who have touched my life in enormously meaningful ways.

A special word of thanks and appreciation to the congregations of the First United Methodist Church of Compton, the Calvary United Methodist Church of Los Angeles, and the Vermont Square United Methodist Church of Los Angeles, who were the "test audiences" for these messages and particularly to those church members who encouraged me to keep preaching on Afrocentric themes.

I wish also to express thanks to Kenneth L. Waters, Jr., age nine, who was content to play basketball downstairs in the church gym by himself while his father labored at the computer.

I finally wish to express my gratitude to Kristy Arnesen Pullen, Patricia Finn, and William Key of Judson Press for their openness to these messages and for their encouragement.

# Introduction

A BOOK OF CHRISTIAN SERMONS solely dedicated to celebrating the history and heritage of Africans born in the Americas has never before been published. While this accounts for the uniqueness of this collection, the reasons for publishing it are more crucial. There has been great injury done to African American people and more trauma continues to be visited upon us. Nowadays, however, the injury is not so much outward and physical as inward and psychological . . . or should we say, spiritual? The point is that great damage has been done to the corporate pride, sense of self-worth, self-esteem, and self-respect of African American people. Surely, the African American experience includes many positive developments in their psychological and spiritual history as a people. There were the glory days of Marcus Garvey (1887–1940), whose Universal Negro Improvement Association (UNIA) promoted a philosophy of African nobility. There was the advent of the American civil rights movement and the Black Revolution, which concurred during the 1950s and 1960s under the respective visions of Martin Luther King, Jr. (1929–1968), and Malcolm X (1925–1965). There were the consciousness-changing cries of "Black Power," "Black is beautiful," "I'm black and I'm proud," and "I am somebody" that attended the African American challenge to the status quo. But as we face the twenty-first century, a considerable number of African Americans stand as though these cries were never uttered. These echoes of pride, self-determination, and identity are less than a faded memory, especially to many younger African Americans. There also appear to be older African Americans who have never embraced the renaissance of cultural pride and identity. It is no mystery what has happened. While the structures of white advantage were to some limited extent breached, the ideology of white supremacy has remained firmly embedded in both secular and religious forms of media, communication, and education. While African Americans have won a measure of freedom for our bodies, too many of our minds remain enslaved by the more subtle manacles of an ideology of white racial preference. The structures of discrimination are now attempting a comeback in updated forms, and African Americans in large measure have not the spirit to respond.

Within the wider community, the white assault upon the African American psyche has yielded the spoiled fruit of gang violence, homicide, drug trafficking, drug use, idleness, despair, domestic violence, crime, alcoholism, suicide, and mental breakdown. These are the symptoms of a people who have been taught self-hate. Within the religious community, this same assault has resulted in a culture of imitating "whiteness." Many African American congregations yearning for acceptance and approval from whites in mainline denominations have forsaken the rich heritage of worship and music in the African American tradition to copy the habits and styles of white Euro-American churches. This too is self-hate. Some black churches so loathe their own heritage that they have cut themselves off from the masses of their own people. Many of these churches are stagnant and declining, with little or no outreach or service to their communities.

As a pastor who has on more than one occasion found himself assigned to struggling black congregations in the midst of crumbling black communities, I have sought ways to heal the spirit of my people so that they can rise up and be the people of God. The challenge has always been to overthrow the effects of years of social programming and to liberate people from the worship of "whiteness" and the derogation of "African-ness." The task has always been to lead my people beyond pretense and

denial to genuine identity and authenticity. I eventually found a re-
source of great promise and effectiveness in the movement called
Afrocentricity.

Afrocentricity is a multidisciplinary program with both schol-
arly and popular approaches designed to rescue African history and
heritage from academic and ideological forced exile. By no means
a brand-new movement, Afrocentric thinking can be discovered
as far back as Frederick Douglass (1817–1895), Henry McNeal
Turner (1839–1915), Mary Church Terrell (1863–1954), Mary
McLeod Bethune (1875–1955), and several of their contemporaries. Afrocentricity has produced an expansive range of art and
literature. It is based upon a worldview that values Africa and persons of African descent and holds them central. This worldview is
solidly supported by evidence from various fields of investigation
including archaeology and paleontology, linguistics, anthropology,
iconography, and historiography.

My challenge as a Christian preacher has been to introduce this
wide breadth of scholarship and information to the people in the
pew and to do so in a way that is palatable and profitable for them.
The sermon series, of course, is a uniquely suitable way of con-
veying the insights of Afrocentric scholarship in relatively short
increments of time over the course of several weeks (Bible studies
and Christian education series are yet other ways). But how does
the preacher craft a particular sermon in a way that would make
reception and retention of this knowledge easy for young and old
alike while at the same time satisfying the basic cultural require-
ment of inspiring the heart? The ten sermons in this book represent
my attempt to answer this question. They were chosen from a thick
file of sermons preached in several congregations, civic organiza-
tions, and professional group meetings over the course of eight
years. Among the audiences were three congregations that I have
pastored. These particular sermons were chosen because of their
representative nature. Together they embrace all the Afrocentric
themes that I have ever tried to address. Furthermore, they each
contribute some peculiar insight not found elsewhere in the series.
Admittedly, the transition from an oral to a printed presentation

required that the sermons be reworked to please the eye, although the imprint of their original oral character may still be detectable. There are themes that recur throughout the series, but repetitious material has been eliminated. Dates and details that would normally be passed over in an oral presentation have been included for the reader's information. The opportunity has been taken to provide notations and a bibliography so that anyone wishing to explore the more technical foundations of these messages will have readily identifiable places to begin.

Response to these sermons in a church setting has been intriguing. Most of my congregants have never heard these matters discussed. The majority are surprised to learn these truths about their history and heritage. Nevertheless, they usually appear deeply appreciative of being told these things for the first time in their lives. In fact, I have seen many people transformed by their knowledge of the black presence in history. I have also seen the black congregation as a whole revitalized as a result of the preaching represented in this book. Several times church members told me that these messages confirmed what they had always felt deep in their hearts.

Still, these sermons are controversial, as is the entire Afrocentricity movement. I therefore anticipate some criticisms of these messages that should be responded to beforehand. The most egregiously hypocritical charge of all would be that these sermons are racist or, in some way, an example of "reverse racism." It has indeed become the vogue for some members of historically oppressive ethnic groups to project their sins upon members of historically oppressed groups. They do this for two reasons: to assuage their guilt and to intimidate those members of the historically oppressed group who would challenge those of the historically oppressive group.

The whole notion of reverse racism, black racism, or any racism other than white racism is illogical, ahistorical, and insubstantial. As I have argued elsewhere, racism is the proactive, unprovoked posture of those possessing, first, a theory of racial superiority, second, the power (economic, political, military, and paramilitary) to force their will upon others, and, third, an established historical and sociological relationship to victims that cannot be "reversed."[1] These sermons are not racist, but anti-racist and counter-racist. They are meant to overthrow and eradicate the *effects* of racism, effects that even the best-meaning white people are often instrumental in perpetuating, however unwillingly. This, by the way, alludes to an incidental benefit of these sermons for white readers. They expose the hidden, unconscious racism of white thinking, language, and imagery, a step that is at least prerequisite if white people ever hope to overcome their racism.

Another charge might be that these sermons are anti-white. Much depends upon what is meant by "white." Does "white" refer to an attitude or a group of people? If "white" means a mindset that would preserve privilege for descendants of Europeans at the expense of descendants of Africans and others, then, yes, these sermons are anti-white. But it would be wrong to characterize these sermons as "anti-white people." They are pro-black and, again, anti-racist, but not anti-white people. I, in fact, know white people who are partners with black people and others in the fight for racial and social justice. Some are theologically conservative, some are theologically liberal, but they all demonstrate progressive thinking in regard to the African American estate in this country. These messages are certainly not against them, nor are they against any well-meaning white person who seeks ways to exterminate the social and psychological disease of racism.

Some would probably say that these sermons are angry and iconoclastic. Merely characterizing them this way would be an attempt to prevent others from taking them seriously. My own hope is that these sermons demonstrate prophetic indignation over what has happened to black people in this country. I hope also that these sermons demonstrate a prophetic passion for the truth. They seek to build up a people who have been torn down, and insofar as they are my people, the work cannot be done dispassionately. Besides, these sermons are not so intense that they preclude humor, a feature that I hope will not be missed.

---

1. Kenneth L. Waters, Sr., "The Myth of Reverse Racism (Or Can Black People Be Racists, Too?)," *The Journal of the Interdenominational Theological Center* 19 (Fall 1991/Spring 1992): 130–150.

Sometimes those of us who espouse an Afrocentric message are accused of being separatists, especially when we expose the subterfuge and dishonesty of those who promote assimilation while pretending to promote "integration," "pluralism," or "multiculturalism." The attitude reflected in these sermons is not separatist, but it is anti-assimilationist. Assimilation can be a program forcibly imposed upon distinct others by members of a dominating ethnic group, however subtly that force may be applied, or, from another perspective, it can be the unwary voluntary acquiescence of a proscribed ethnic group. The former may be called active assimilation or cultural chauvinism; the latter may be called passive assimilation or cultural surrender. In either case, the cultural heritage of the proscribed group is suppressed or forfeited in favor of that of the dominating group. In *genuine* "integration," "pluralism," or "multiculturalism," the cultural heritage of no group is suppressed or lost, but rather the heritage of each group is augmented, enriched, and informed through intercultural sharing and borrowing. Because our desire is for *genuine* celebration of diversity, it is important for people of African descent to be clear about the heritage that is ours. We cannot preserve, protect, or share, nor will any other people appreciate what we fail to acknowledge as our own.

In regard to more substantive matters, some may question my use of the word "black" as a descriptive term for certain peoples and personalities in biblical and classical times. They may see my use of the word "black" as anachronistic or as an attempt to retroject a twentieth-century concept into an ancient mind-set. My response to possible objections to my use of the word "black" will give me an opportunity to provide a theoretical and historical base for the sermons that follow. First, I should offer a definition. My word "black" as a descriptive term for both ancient and modern peoples and personalities refers to those having an African bloodline with *any* combination or degree of discernible African features. By "discernible African features" I mean those physical traits generally associated with the first indigenous inhabitants of African lands and their most direct descendants (e.g., dark skin, coarse or curly hair, and broad or full facial features).

There are those who deny the blackness of certain ancient African and Asian populations, even though an African bloodline among these populations is nearly undeniable. In light of this, my insistence upon a definition for blackness that includes "discernible African features" may at first appear to some Afrocentric thinkers as too much of a concession to our detractors. From a polemical point of view, it would be more advantageous to insist upon a faithful and consistent application of traditional American standards of "blackness" such as used by the U.S. Bureau of the Census and some American municipalities. According to these standards, individuals are "black" even if they possess measures of genetic mix as minuscule as "one drop" of African blood or "one-sixteenth" of African ancestry.[2] Truly, if we accept these standards then we have done enough to easily establish the black African identity of the overwhelming majority of populations in the ancient Mediterranean world. Indeed, after reading the multivolume classic on race-mixing by Joel A. Rogers (1883–1966),[3] one is inclined, on the basis of these standards, to declare the black identity of the overwhelming majority of populations in modern Europe, America, Asia, and the peoples of the islands of the Atlantic, the Pacific, and the Caribbean. However, for clarity's sake and for the sake of the message proclaimed throughout these sermons, I think that it is best to draw a slightly more restrictive line on who should be declared black in ancient and modern times. To include "any combination or degree of discernible African features" in our understanding of blackness would draw the line in this way. Furthermore, I do not believe that by advocating this understanding of blackness we would be conceding too much. After all, we are speaking of *any combination or degree* of "discernible African features." In Amsterdam, I saw very dark-skinned black people with naturally straight hair and "Nordic" facial features, while back home in Los Angeles I see black people with very pronounced

---

2. See the comments on the "one-drop" idea in Walter Arthur McCray, *The Black Presence in the Bible: Discovering the Black and African Identity of Biblical Persons and Nations* (Chicago: Black Light Fellowship, 1990), pp. 14–15, 150–151. See also J. A. Rogers, *World's Great Men of Color*, vol. 1, with an introduction by John Henrik Clarke (New York: Collier Books-Macmillan Publishing Co., 1972), p. 13.

3. See the Bibliography.

"Negroid" features yet with skin tone lighter than that of some white people. I personally know black people who could pass and have passed for white whose African features are barely discernible, but discernible nevertheless to anyone who knows what to look for. My definition allows for this much variety in our understanding of blackness and, since it does, I would argue that it is hardly less advantageous than the American "one-drop" standard.

Ultimately, the issue of how restrictive or advantageous my definition may be is moot because the evidence of ancient witnesses indicates that the ancient peoples and personalities referred to as black in these pages were visibly black to a high degree. By this I mean that if their identical twins had appeared in the American South of the 1940s, 1950s, and 1960s these look-alikes would have been required to wait for their bus in the "colored section" of the station waiting room.

One of the most often quoted witnesses to the black African identity of ancient peoples is the Greek historian Herodotus (484?–425? B.C.E.),[4] particularly in regard to his writing *Euterpe,* on the black African identity of the "European" Colchians, and, by implication, the Egyptians and the Ethiopians:

> There can be no doubt that the Colchians are an Egyptian race.... My own conjectures were founded, first, on the fact that they are black-skinned and have wooly hair, which certainly amounts to but little, since several other nations are so too; but further ... the Colchians, the Egyptians, and the Ethiopians, are the only nations that have practiced circumcision from the earliest times.[5]

When the word "race" appears in an English translation of an ancient text, as it does above, then it is best understood as a synonym for "nation."

---

4. "B.C.E." (before the common era) and "C.E." (of the common era) are used in this work instead of the more traditional "B.C." and "A.D."

5. *Euterpe* 104.69, *The History of Herodotus,* trans. George Rawlinson (Chicago: Encyclopedia Britannica, 1952), p. 69; quoted in John G. Jackson, *Introduction to African Civilizations,* with an introduction by John Henrik Clarke (Secaucus, N.J.: Citadel Press, 1970), p. 92.

Ammianus Marcellinus (c. 330–c. 400 C.E.), a Roman historian writing at a much later time, offers a rather unflattering but informative portrait of the Egyptians of his day:

> Now the men of Egypt are, as a rule, somewhat swarthy and dark of complexion, and rather gloomy-looking, slender and hardy, excitable in all their movements, quarrelsome, and most persistent duns."[6]

The Greek historian Diodorus of Sicily (c. 57 B.C.E.) tells us that the majority of Ethiopians in Egypt, Arabia, Libya, and along the river banks of North Africa are "black in color and have flat noses and wooly hair."[7]

The Greek historian and geographer Strabo (b. 64 B.C.E.?) also refers to "the black complexion and wooly hair of the Aethiopians."[8] Strabo also tells us that the people of southern India are "like the Aethiopians in color" although their hair is straight because of the "humidity," while the Indians in the north have curly hair more like the Egyptians.[9] These and other ancient populations (as we shall see) were visibly black according to our understanding of blackness today. This is not to deny that there were members of these nations and separate African nations altogether whose indigenous African characteristics were not as pronounced. A statement made by Chancellor Williams is instructive:

> *All unmixed* Africans are not jet black. For while the great majority are black skinned, countless thousands who lived for centuries in cool areas have lighter complexion — and no "Caucasian blood" at all.[10]

Obviously, indigenous African peoples in the ancient world were various shades of black, ranging from the light brown of some

---

6. *Julianus* 22.16, 23, *Ammianus Marcellinus*, vol. 2, trans. John C. Rolfe, Loeb Classical Library Series (Cambridge: Harvard University Press, 1950), p. 309; partially quoted in J. A. Rogers, *World's Great Men of Color*, pp. 119–120.

7. *Book 3* 6.7–8, *Diodorus of Sicily*, vol. 2, trans. C. H. Oldfather, Loeb Classical Library Series (Cambridge: Harvard University Press, 1953), pp. 103–104.

8. *The Geography of Strabo* 15.1.24, vol. 7, trans. Horace Leonard Jones, Loeb Classical Library Series (Cambridge: Harvard University Press, 1954), p. 39.

9. Ibid., 15.1.13, p. 21.

10. Chancellor Williams, *The Destruction of Black Civilization: Great Issues of a Race from 4500 B.C. to 2000 A.D.* (Chicago: Third World Press, 1987), p. 34.

Egyptians to the deep dark of many Ethiopians. Still, they were all visibly "black," as the ancient testimonies show. Therefore, our application of the descriptive term "black" to certain ancient peoples and personalities is not at all strained. Furthermore, even though the word "African," as I use it, always denotes a dark-skinned indigenous inhabitant of an African land, I shall retain the phrase "black African" as a necessary redundancy in order to help counter a tendency in historical studies to represent the persons and nations in question as "white Africans."

Still, there are those who would object to my application of the term "black" by saying, first of all, that there were no categories or classifications of race (i.e., Negroid, Mongoloid, and Caucasoid) in ancient times.[11] People did not refer to themselves or to other people in terms of skin color (black, brown, red, yellow, or white). Indeed, people referred to themselves and to others in terms of nationality (Egyptian, Ethiopian, Jew, Assyrian, Greek, Roman, etc.) without regard to physical traits such as skin color.[12] This argument is good as far as it goes. However, some of those who argue these points would further say that my use of the word "black" as a descriptive term is retrojecting a modern term onto an ancient mind-set, an anachronism. To show that this is not the case I must first make clear that people in antiquity actually identified themselves and others in at least three ways: first, according to that

---

11. These terms (along with "Australoid") were fashioned by Ashley Montagu, editor of *The Concept of Race* (New York: Free Press of Glencoe, 1968) and author of *Man's Most Dangerous Myth: The Fallacy of Race*, 5th ed. (New York: Oxford University Press, 1974). Although Montagu classified humankind into four "major groups," he rejected the concept of "race." Carolus Linnaeus, author of *Systema Naturae* (1735), further divided the human species into six varieties. The word "race" as a synonym of "kind" or "variety" was used by Comte Georges Louis LeClerc de Buffon, author of *Histoire naturelle générale et particulier* (1749). But it was the influence of Charles Darwin (1809–1882), author of *On the Origin of Species* (1859) and *The Descent of Man* (1871), that invested the concept of race with a modern meaning (i.e., distinct, separately evolved species of human beings) and that laid the groundwork for the development of theories of racial superiority and inferiority. C. S. Coon, author of *The Origin of the Races* (New York: Alfred A. Knopf, 1968), popularized the Darwinian concept of race, but not without protest from the scientific community. For a discussion of these matters see Michael Bradley, *The Iceman Inheritance: Prehistoric Sources of Western Man's Racism, Sexism, and Aggression* (New York: Warner Books, 1978), pp. 32–58; reprint edition, with an introduction by John Henrik Clarke (New York: Kayode Publications, 1991), pp. 193–211.

12. See Frank J. Yurco, "Were the Ancient Egyptians Black or White?" *Biblical Archaeology Review* 15, no. 5 (September/October 1989): 24–29, 58.

accidental aspect of their identity resulting from birth and/or up-
bringing in a specific locale or culture; second, according to that
aspect of their identity resulting from the choice to live in and
abide by the rules of a specific locale or culture; and, third, according to that aspect of their identity resulting from physical and
cultural characteristics that they shared in common with distant
others who were indigenous in predominant numbers to a specific
locale.

The first aspect of ancient identity may be called "ethnicity"
(Greek: *ethnos* = nation), the second, "citizenship," and the third,
"ancestry." Ethnicity and citizenship may be understood as forms
of national identity, the former by birth, the latter by choice, while
ancestry may be understood as the national origins of a people or
person's forebears, however distant in chronology and geography
those origins may be from that people or person's actual birthplace
and culture. Sometimes there is a very fine and fluid line between
ethnicity and ancestry, especially when there has never been any
migration beyond the birth environment, but for the purposes of
this discussion the term "ancestry" implies some remoteness on the
part of people and individuals from their forebears' birthplace and
culture.

Although certain physical traits tended to be dominant among
specific ethnic groups in the ancient Mediterranean world, these
traits were not really essential for having a specific ethnic identity. A people's ethnicity was constituted more by their inherited
stock of traditions (language, worldview, lifestyle, art forms, values, habits, customs, taboos, etc.) than by their physical traits.
Citizenship in ancient times had even less connection to the physical characteristics that we today would associate with "race." While
ethnicity was mainly birth identity, citizenship was mainly an identity received from or bestowed by a governmental-political entity
(e.g., the Roman empire). Paul the apostle (d. 65 C.E.), for example, identified himself in terms of both his ethnicity as a Jew
and his citizenship as a Roman, depending upon which was more
convenient at the time (Acts 21:39; 22:25-29). Augustine (354–
430 C.E.), bishop of Hippo, lived for a while as a Roman citizen
in Rome and Milan, yet acknowledged his ethnic identity as an

African.[13] Septimus Severus (146–211 C.E.) was of ethnic African (Carthaginian) descent, yet he was a Roman citizen. In fact, he was emperor of Rome! He was no hero to the early church yet an important example of the powerful African presence in the ancient Roman empire.[14] Clitus (c. 300 B.C.E.), a general in the army of Alexander the Great and, later, king of Bactria (now northern Afghanistan and eastern Iran), although politically a Macedonian, was ethnically a North African.[15] Whether by present ethnicity or distant ancestry, Augustine, Septimus Severus, and Clitus were North Africans regardless of their citizenship. We come now to the matter of ancestry.

Statements by Herodotus, Ammianus, Diodorus, and Strabo, such as those we have already considered, show us that people in the ancient world nevertheless recognized and acknowledged distinctive physical characteristics that belonged to particular peoples who were indigenous in predominant numbers to specific geographical areas. Consequently, certain sets of physical characteristics were *associated* with certain ethnic groups, even though these characteristics were never ascribed more than superficial importance nor were they thought of as necessary for anyone to possess a particular ethnic identity. When these physical characteristics were observed in a people or individual who was distantly removed in time and space from the geographical area where these characteristics were dominant, then these characteristics were taken as indicators, not of "race" as we understand it today, but of ancestral national origins or, simply, ancestry.

Perhaps our most famous example of this is, again, Herodotus's attempt to postulate the ancestry of the Colchians (located on the eastern shore of the Black Sea in the present-day former U.S.S.R.)

13. *Confessions,* book 8.6, *Saint Augustine: Confessions,* trans. R. S. Pine-Coffin (New York: Penguin Books, 1978), p. 166.

14. Yosef A. A. ben-Jochannan, *African Origins of the Major "Western Religions"* (Baltimore: Black Classic Press, 1991), p. 79. Compare the contrasting view in Michael Grant, *The Roman Emperors: A Biographical Guide to the Rulers of Imperial Rome (31 B.C.–A.D. 476)* (New York: Charles Scribner's Sons, 1985), pp. 112–113.

15. Diodorus of Sicily *Book 17* 20.7; 56.57, *Diodorus of Sicily,* vol. 8, trans. C. Bradford Welles, Loeb Classical Library Series (Cambridge: Harvard University Press, 1968), pp. 177, 281. Diodorus refers to him as Clitus the Black (Greek: *ho melas*). See also J. A. Rogers, *World's Great Men of Color,* pp. 94–97.

as an "Egyptian race" based first upon their common physical characteristics (black skin and wooly hair) and then upon their common practice of circumcision. Incidentally, Diodorus of Sicily addresses the belief that the Egyptians are a "colony" of the Ethiopians for a variety of reasons having to do with their similarities in customs, craftwork, and lettering.[16] Although Diodorus does not mention similarities in physical characteristics between the Egyptians and the Ethiopians, his statements are consistent with the ancient belief expressed by Herodotus and others that the Egyptians and the Ethiopians are ethnically *and* physically one people.

In other cases, identity with an ancestral nation on the basis of physical (and cultural) characteristics was implied. The Old Testament Scriptures refer to the black African ancestry of the original inhabitants of the Judean wilderness by saying "the former inhabitants there belonged to Ham" (1 Chronicles 4:40, RSV). Interestingly, by the time of David the king (1000–962 B.C.E.) there was still a people of black African ancestry called the Jebusites (Genesis 10:16) inhabiting the area that became Jerusalem (1 Chronicles 11:4-9). Tacitus (c. 55–117 C.E.), the Roman historian, implies that the early Jews were so African in their appearance that many people thought the Jews "were a race of Ethiopian origin."[17] Strabo reports that in his day the prevailing opinion was that the ancestors of the Jews were the Egyptians.[18] Incidentally, in the Tacitus text there is also confusion over the geographical origins of the Jews, but the only case of possible confusion in regard to their "racial" ancestry is over their identity as Ethiopians. The fact that the ancients identified the Jews with both Egyptians and Ethiopians speaks, of course, to the black African identity of the early Jews, especially because such identifications seem to be based largely upon physical appearances. Therefore, when I speak of ancient people and persons as "black" I am not making a statement about how they thought of themselves nor about how their contemporaries thought of them, but rather about how they were or

---

16. *Book 3* 3.2, *Diodorus of Sicily*, vol. 2, p. 95.
17. *History* 5.2, *The Complete Works of Tacitus*, trans. Alfred John Church and William Jackson Brodribb (New York: Random House, 1942), pp. 657–658.
18. *The Geography of Strabo* 16.2.34, vol. 7, p. 281.

would have been *described* by ancient eyewitnesses, and identified, in some cases, in terms of ancestry. I am also indicating how they would be identified by us today despite their self-understanding. Thus I feel that by using the word "black" simply as a descriptive term, with no reference to ancient self-understanding, I am avoiding retrojection of present-day understandings onto an ancient mind-set.

Parenthetically, we should also acknowledge that since there were in ancient times no categories of race as we understand it there was also no racism as we understand it, i.e., theories of racial superiority and inferiority. As we do not wish to retroject the modern concept of race into ancient times, we also do not wish to retroject the modern issue of racism. Since there is some confusion on this point I should clarify further. There were cases of color-based hostility in ancient times; these hostilities, however, were not predicated upon theories of racial superiority or inferiority, but rather upon territorial disputes and religious differences. Joel A. Rogers called this hostility "color prejudice."[19] Rogers explained that the earliest occurrences of "color prejudice" may have been around 1500 B.C.E., when white-skinned people from beyond the Himalaya Mountains invaded the Indus River Valley (modern Pakistan and India) and clashed with the black-skinned inhabitants there who became known as the Dravidians. These invaders were the people who became known as Indo-Aryans. Rogers's evidence was hostile anti-black statements found in the Indo-Aryan sacred writings (the Vedas, or Hindu Scriptures). Rig-Veda, for example, declares how Indra, the Indo-Aryan national god, hated "black skins."[20]

Rogers also considers North Africa, where Egyptologist Gerald Kennedy discovered hieroglyphical exchanges of hostility between some Egyptians and some even darker-skinned Ethiopians during periods of political discontent. Rogers does not give great weight to these in light of the high degree of admixture between ancient

---

19. J. A. Rogers, *Nature Knows No Color-Line: Research into the Negro Ancestry in the White Race* (St. Petersburg: Helga M. Rogers, 1952; reprint edition 1980), pp. 7–8.
20. Book 9, Hymn 42.1, in ibid.

Egyptians and Ethiopians.[21] Rogers suggested that the rabbis of the first-century C.E. stood next to the Indo-Aryans in degree of "color prejudice." It should be emphasized that Rogers attributed early Jewish expressions of color prejudice to religious, political, and territorial disputes with darker-skinned people, particularly the Egyptians, rather than to feelings of racial superiority. The rabbis, Rogers observed, were themselves dark-skinned, even "black." Nevertheless, it is in the rabbinical (Talmudic) writings that we first find black skin color (i.e., the generally darker color of the Egyptians and the Ethiopians) attributed to a curse that Noah allegedly placed upon his son Ham.[22] Charles Copher has also examined Talmudic writings (i.e., *Sanhedrin* 108b, *Tanhuma Noah* 13, 15 and *Midrash Rabbah*, Genesis 22:6) and discovered, along with legends of Noah cursing Ham, further legends about God's curse upon Cain as the cause of black-skinned humanity.[23]

These occurrences of color-based hostility were very rare and sparsely spread throughout ancient times and different enough in nature from modern racism to warrant being called by a different name. Still, it cannot be denied that there is a connection between a few of these early manifestations of color-based hostility and racism as it developed in post-Darwinian Europe and America. The "curse of Ham" legend was frequently deployed in white pulpits and classrooms of the American South and elsewhere during the era of the Atlantic slave trade (1505–1863) and American chattel slavery (1619–1865). Perhaps the greatest value of this discussion is that it helps us better to understand the mind-set of ancient black people. Since there was no racism to assault their psyches as they matured into adults, they were devoid of any feelings of racial inferiority and racial self-hate. Although many of us born and raised in twentieth-century America cannot say the same thing about ourselves, the self-esteem of our ancient forebears remain a model of pride for us.

---

21. Ibid., pp. 8–9.
22. Ibid., pp. 9–16.
23. Charles B. Copher, "The Black Presence in the Old Testament," *Stony the Road We Trod: African American Biblical Interpretation,* ed. Cain Hope Felder (Minneapolis: Fortress Press, 1991), pp. 146–164.

These sermons and other Afrocentric approaches to the Bible and to history are made necessary partly because black people of African descent have been largely erased from history. However, a final complaint after reading these pages might be that we have now erased white people from history! Addressing this matter will also give me an opportunity to provide a historical background for these sermons.

There were white Asians (Eurasians) and white Europeans in ancient Northeast Africa and Southwest Asia, but they had been a significant and controlling political presence in these regions only from the seventh century B.C.E. (c. 661 B.C.E.).[24] From 4000 B.C.E. wars were fought in which the indigenous Africans of Upper Egypt (southern Egypt and the Sudan on modern maps) repelled invading Eurasian armies, driving them back to Lower Egypt (northern Egypt on modern maps). Some Eurasians were taken as prisoners of war and slaves, beginning the process of Eurasian integration into black Egyptian culture on a relatively small scale. There was larger-scale integration of Eurasians into black Upper Egypt after 3100 B.C.E., when the Nubian-Egyptian pharaoh Menes I conquered and annexed Lower Egypt (which, by the way, was still predominantly black).[25] Settlements of non-militant Eurasian immigrants were subsequently allowed around the northeastern edges of First Dynasty Egypt, which not only led to intercultural trade and commerce between blacks and whites but also to concubinage and intermarriage between the immigrant and indigenous populations.

There is a regrettable tendency in historical studies to ascribe the ascendency and achievements of ancient black civilizations both African and Asian to the presence of white Asian or white European "elements" in those civilizations. This is a grave error. As consistently demonstrated by scholars of ancient Africa both black and white, black civilization, particularly Ethiopia and Egypt and their satellites (i.e., Mesopotamia and India) had reached the highest levels of development, far surpassing white Asian and white

---

24. See Chancellor Williams, *The Destruction of Black Civilization*, pp. 39–43, 96–120. See also John G. Jackson, *Introduction to African Civilizations*, pp. 97–121.

25. See Ibid.

European nations of the same period centuries before first contact with whites.[26] The entry of foreign elements into the social and ethnic bloodlines of North Africa engendered some tensions, conflicts, and even resentment against the government that allowed it, but biologically and politically North Africa remained black-ruled and black-dominated.

There was a significant white encroachment upon black North Africa in the invasion, triumph, and subsequent rule of the Asiatic Hyksos (1720–1540 B.C.E.), but war was declared upon them by Pharaoh Kamose of Thebes (1645–1567 B.C.E.), and by 1540 B.C.E., the Hyksos were finally defeated and expelled from Egypt by Pharaoh Ahmose I, brother of Kamose (c. 1570 B.C.E.), and Queen Nefertari I (c. 1570 B.C.E.).[27] Black dominance was thus regained.

The beginning of the end of black political dominance in North Africa is marked by the Assyrian invasion and destruction of the city of Thebes in 661 B.C.E.. The later conquest and rule of Egypt by the Persians (525–330 B.C.E.) under Darius the Great and his sons, the Greek invasion of Egypt under Alexander the Great (332 B.C.E.), and the continuation of Greek domination under the Ptolemies (323–31 B.C.E.) furthered the decline and near demise of black African civilization.

Meanwhile, the Romans had defeated the forces of the African city-state of Carthage on three occasions (the Punic, or Carthaginian, Wars), first in 242 B.C.E., when the Romans, assisted by the Macedonian Ptolemy II Philadelphus (308–246 B.C.E.), repelled the forces of the Carthaginian general Hamilcar Barca (d. 228 B.C.E.) from Sicily; second, in 202 B.C.E., when the Roman general Cornelius Scipio Africanus (234?–183 B.C.E.) finally defeated the Carthaginian general Hannibal, son of Hamilcar Barca (247–182 B.C.E., in Zama (in present-day Algeria), and subsequently attacked Carthage itself; and finally in 146 B.C.E., when Roman

---

26. See Cheikh Anta Diop, *The African Origin of Civilization: Myth or Reality?* trans. Mercer Cook (Westport, Conn.: Lawrence Hill and Co., 1974), pp. 152–153; see also Chancellor Williams, *The Destruction of Black Civilization,* p. 296.

27. Chancellor Williams, *The Destruction of Black Civilization,* pp. 39–43, 96–120; John G. Jackson, *Introduction to African Civilizations,* pp. 97–121.

armies, commanded by Cato the Elder (a member of the Roman Senate) intervened in a Carthaginian attack upon their ally King Masinissa (238–149 B.C.E.) of Numidia, and afterward destroyed the city of Carthage and its great library.[28] Rome, led by Augustus Caesar (63 B.C.E.–14 C.E.), the first Roman emperor, finally advanced upon Egypt in 31 B.C.E., defeating the forces of the Egyptian queen Cleopatra VII (69–30 B.C.E.) and her ally, the Roman Mark Anthony (83–30 B.C.E.).

After these invasions, North Africa was never to recover its former stature among world civilizations. History would repeat itself to some extent in the ascent of great West African civilizations like Ghana, Mali, Songhay, the Mossi states, the Hausa states, and Congo (700–1500 C.E.) and their subsequent decline and near demise (1505–1863 C.E.) under the assault of the Portuguese, British, French, Dutch, Americans, Spanish, Belgians, and Italians. This brief account of the white presence in ancient African history serves, of course, to explain Africa's fall from its ancient glory and to illustrate, contrary to what we may have been told, that this fall was not due to any inherent deficiency in the African soul.

With these defenses of my position in place, I present these sermons on "the beauty of blackness in the Bible." There is a tradition in black preaching known as "calling the ro'" in which preachers conclude their messages with a series of witnesses from the Bible. I would like to conclude this introduction with one witness from elsewhere. Philo of Alexandria (c. 20 B.C.E.–50 C.E.), the Jewish philosopher, said that when God created the body of the first man that God "painted it with a dark hue desiring the first man to be as beautiful as possible."[29] Therefore, when we proclaim the "beauty of blackness" we are not doing anything new or modern. No, we stand in the very old and august tradition (date of writing c. 960 B.C.E.) of the Song of Solomon 1:5 — "I am black and beautiful" (NRSV) — which surely antedates even the ancient African Philo.

---

28. J. A. Rogers, *World's Great Men of Color,* vol. 1, pp. 98–107, 110–117.
29. Philo, *On the Creation of the World* 47.138; cf. "rich complexion" in *Philo,* vol. 1, trans. F. H. Colson and G. H. Whitaker, Loeb Classical Library Series (Cambridge: Harvard University Press, 1971), p. 109.

# Made in God's Image

### Genesis 1:26-31; 2:7 and Ezekiel 1:26-28

I WANT TO BE CLEAR that when I speak of being made in the image of God I am speaking of being made in God's spiritual image, not God's physical image. As creatures of God, we are made in the spiritual image of God, which means that we have qualities and attributes that are like the qualities and attributes of God. Still, even though I am speaking of being made in God's spiritual image, I cannot help but be impressed by our Scripture text from the book of Ezekiel.

In this text, Ezekiel the prophet (c. 592 B.C.E.) has a vision of God in much the same way that other men and women have had visions of God, but what is interesting to us is the way that Ezekiel describes his vision. Ezekiel says that he saw God sitting upon a throne in the form of a human being. He then goes on to say that God's upper body was like bronze encased in fire. In other words, Ezekiel the prophet is declaring that he saw God in the form of a man with bronze-colored skin.

In the book of the prophet Daniel (7:9), we have another vision of God. This time the prophet again describes God in the form of a human being seated on a throne. God's clothes were as white as snow. There is no reference to God's skin color, but the prophet says that the hair on God's head was like pure wool — referring to lamb's wool. Now, some will say that the prophet is here referring only to the color of the Lord's hair, but many of us have come to realize that when the prophet says that the Lord's hair is like lamb's wool, he is speaking not only of the color of the Lord's hair but also of its texture.

The visions of Ezekiel and Daniel are echoed in the book of Revelation (1:12-16), where we have the apostle John's vision of the glorified Lord (and as far as we are concerned, Ezekiel, Daniel, and John were seeing the same divine person). In the book of Revelation, we have the Lord again described as a human being or a "son of man." Again, the Lord's white hair is said to be as wool and his feet like burnished bronze refined in a fire. It is interesting that in the book of Ezekiel, the Lord's upper body was the color of bronze, while in the book of Revelation the Lord's feet were the color of bronze — which makes sense, since most people's feet are normally the same color as the rest of their body. Therefore, when we study the descriptions of the way God reveals the Divine Self to the prophets and to the apostle John, we get a unified picture of God in the form of a human being with bronze skin and short curly hair. In other words, the appearance of God to the prophets and the apostle is like that of an African black man.

"Well, Pastor, are you saying that God is black?" Why not? Where do we get this idea that just because God is Spirit that God is colorless? Where does the idea of the colorless, shapeless, featureless God come from? Why would God, who made the colors and called them good, deny Godself of color? Yes, God is invisible to us, but must that mean that God is a formless, characterless, colorless heavenly haze? Why is it that as long as God is pictured as a grandfatherly white man with a long flowing beard, the way that Michelangelo Buonarroti (1475–1554 C.E.) portrayed God on the ceiling of the Sistine Chapel, nobody raises any question, nobody gets upset? But when someone suggests that God may be more appropriately pictured as black, we suddenly hear this chorus of protest saying, "No, God has no color!" It is as if we are being told, "Either God is white or God has no color at all, but God definitely cannot be black."

Nevertheless, the Bible does specify a color for God, particularly in the form in which God is revealed to human beings. When God *revealed* Godself to Ezekiel and to John and, I am sure, even to Daniel, God was *revealed* as a person of dark color. We have no way yet of knowing what God really looks like, but on the basis of the Bible we at least know that God revealed Godself as a dark-skinned human being. We need not argue about what color God really is. Let us just settle on the way God was revealed in the Scriptures. I am saying that God revealed the Divine Self in the form of an African black man.

Is this farfetched? Why doesn't someone ask, "Is the idea of God as a white European farfetched?" Also, why doesn't someone ask, "Are these portraits of Jesus, hanging on our walls, depicting him as a blue-eyed white man with flowing blond hair farfetched?" Why doesn't someone ask, "Are the pictures in our Sunday school literature representing ancient Near Easterners as white Europeans farfetched?" If anything is farfetched, it is the notion that the majority of people in ancient Africa and the ancient Near East were blue-eyed blond white people.

But to answer the question, no, the idea of God *revealed* as an African black man is not farfetched. We must realize that the world of the Old and New Testaments was not a white-European world (nor a Greco-Roman world in the specific case of the New Testament) but an African-Asian world. All we have to do is get out a map of Bible lands and look at how close all the places of the Bible are to Africa. Some of them are *in* Africa. The people of the biblical world of the ancient Near East were an African-Asian people, and more African than anything else. It only makes sense that when God chose to reveal Godself to one of the inhabitants of the land that God would be revealed as one of them, as an African. There is something in this that says how much God loves us as an African people. There is something in this that says how much God values us as an African people. God loves and values us so much that God is willing to be revealed as one of us — that is, if God does not already look like us.

I know that this is hard for many of us to accept. We have been taught and some of us have believed that everything good, everything powerful, and everything worthy must be white. To suggest that the One who is Goodness Itself, Power Itself, and Worth Itself is also black is, for many of us, a shock to our psyches. So let me just shift to the question of what it means to be made in

God's image. Regardless of what God really looks like, regardless of whether God has color or no color, what does it mean to be made in God's image?

To be made in God's image means that we are spiritual creatures. "Then the Lord God formed man of dust from the ground, and breathed into his nostrils the breath of life; and man became a living being" (Genesis 2:7, RSV; cf. "living soul," KJV). This means that the source of our lives is the breath of God or, in other words, the Spirit of God; and the way we stay alive is by keeping ourselves open to the Spirit of God. There are many today who are breathing, walking around, and doing things, but still they are dead, dead on the inside, because they are not open to the life-giving Spirit of God. To be open to the Spirit of God means that we are ready to welcome the Spirit when the Spirit comes. It means that we are able to feel the Spirit when the Spirit comes. It means that we will be guided by the Spirit when the Spirit comes. It means that we are ready to respond to the Spirit when the Spirit comes.

In too many of our churches, we who are of African descent have shut out the Spirit in an effort to imitate the European worship style of many white people. Some of our black worship services are so dead and cold that by the time we have walked down the aisle to take our seats, icicles are hanging off us. In these churches, the music is dead and dry. The people are rigid and stiff. It is so quiet that we can hear a pin drop on the carpet. Nobody says, "Amen," nobody shouts "hallelujah," nobody lifts her arms in praise, nobody claps his hands, nobody taps her feet, nobody sheds a tear. This is not "our" worship. Worship in the African tradition is rhythmic, expressive, spiritual worship. Worship in the African tradition is worship we can feel until we can't keep still. Worship in the African tradition is worship that sets our hearts on fire. Worship in the African tradition is worship that makes noise. Worship in the African tradition is worship that makes us get up and move.

I find it interesting that when I travel around the church preaching, I often find myself in the midst of white people who say to me, "We are tired of being cold and dead. We want some life in our churches." I have been among white people who raise their hands in praise, white people who shout "Amen" in church, white people who move and dance. And then when I come home to my people, we are cold and dead. Something is wrong here. Here we are trying to act like them, there they are trying to act like us. We, who are black, need to stop being ashamed of our own worship tradition. We need to stop being ashamed of our own African spirituality. It is true that we, who were born and raised in America, are not as African as our indigenous brothers and sisters. We have been "Americanized." We have been "Europeanized." As W. E. B. Du Bois (1868–1963) said, there is a "twoness" in our identity.[1] But we need not cast out the African for the American or the European. Let us just be ourselves.

To be made in the image of God also means that we are social creatures. "Then God said, 'Let us make man in our image, after our likeness'" (Genesis 1:26, RSV). Who was the "us" that God was referring to? Some Bible scholars say that it was God and the heavenly host. Others say that it was the Father, Son, and Holy Spirit. I personally have no difficulty believing that it was all of the above. Regardless of who the "us" were, the creation of the human being was a social event. The creation of humanity was the work of a social being. It is no wonder, then, that we are also social beings. We are meant to dwell together in community. We are meant to dwell together in relationship to one another.

In African and African American society we have a heritage of community and relationship to one another. It is a heritage rooted in the precolonial social solidarity of the West African nation-states.[2] It is a heritage rooted in the antebellum kinship code of the slave quarters.[3] It is a heritage rooted in the bonds of black brotherhood and sisterhood that held us together in the aftermath of the Civil War. In this heritage, every old man is our father; every young man is our brother. In this heritage, every old woman is our

---

1. W. E. B. Du Bois, *The Souls of Black Folk* with introductions by Dr. Nathan Hare and Alvin F. Poussaint, M.D. (New York: Penguin Books, 1982), p. 45.

2. One of the ways historians and others have diminished the grandeur of African and Native American civilizations is by referring to them as "tribes" and to their leaders as "chiefs," while referring to European civilizations as "nations," "kingdoms," and "states," and to their leaders as "kings," "presidents," and "governors."

3. See John W. Blassingame, *The Slave Community: Plantation Life in the Antebellum South* (New York: Oxford University Press, 1979), pp. 105–106.

mother; every young woman is our sister. In this heritage, every boy child is our son; every girl child is our daughter. In this heritage no one goes without, because the rest of the community is there to share and provide. In this heritage no one is poor, because the wealth of the community belongs to everyone. In this heritage no one is alone, because everyone else in the community is family and friend.

I remember growing up as a child in my community. We had a mother on every corner. If we did anything wrong, there was always someone there to catch us in the act and discipline us. And by the time we got home, word had traveled back that we had been in trouble, and we would be disciplined all over again. I remember hard times, when my family's resources ran low, and we would draw upon the rest of the community to sustain us. There were times when we needed a hand. There were times when we would lend a hand. We were community. We were Africans in America.

But now something has happened to us. We have become too assimilated. We have become too white in our thinking and our behavior. The traditional ideas of community and cooperation have been replaced with the ideas of individualism and competition. Instead of pulling for one another we are pulling against one another. Instead of helping one another get ahead, we are trying to get ahead of one another at the other's expense. Instead of helping one another "get over," we are trying to "get over" on one another. Instead of being there for one another, we are avoiding one another. The image of God in us has been corrupted, and we need to restore it.

This is why we should strive to recover our African heritage. This is why we should strive to uncover our history as an African people. Our lives depend upon it. The image of God within us depends upon it. As long as we deny our heritage and hate who we are, we are destroying ourselves. We are an African people. This means that we are also a social people. To be what we ought to be and to be what God wants us to be, we must become family again, we must become community again, we must become one people again. Black men helping black women, black women helping black men, and all of us helping our children. This is the way it must be.

To be made in the image of God also means that we are creative creatures. "And God blessed them, and God said to them, Be fruitful, and multiply, and fill the earth, and subdue it" (Genesis 1:28, RSV). One of the ways in which we are like God is that we create. Not only do we create children, but we also create families to nurture those children, and then we create communities to sustain those families, and then we create civilizations to sustain those communities. This does not mean that we have become gods. It only means that we are made in the likeness of God.

One of the most damaging lies to be forced upon black people is that we have not created anything of lasting and universal worth, that we have made no significant contribution to humanity nor to world civilization. We have been told that we were only primitives or savages who were "saved" when white people came to Africa, turned us into slaves in America, and "civilized" us. And now everything we have, so they tell us, comes from white people. According to some of them, they built this country — this country that they stole from red people and built up upon the broken backs of black people — and that we owe them for the benefits of culture that they have so graciously bequeathed to us. This is a falsehood that has affected us all of our lives.

As a child growing up in an "integrated" school system, not once was I taught about the great kingdoms and civilizations of North, West, or Central Africa. Not once was I taught about the African contribution to world civilization and culture both ancient and modern. Not once was I taught about the great scholars, scientists, and artists of Africa. I did not even hear about the great men and women of African descent who survived slavery and struggled to live and achieve in America.

But now the truth can be told, and I, for one, feel constrained to tell it. Black people have been the most creative people on the face of the earth, and it was from us — our African forefathers and foremothers — that the world learned everything that has to do with culture and civilization.

We were the first civilizations. I am talking about the cities of Thebes (2050–661 B.C.E.) and Memphis (3100 B.C.E.) in ancient Egypt and the West African empires of Ghana (700–1200 C.E.),

Mali (1200–1500 C.E.), and Songhay (1350–1600 C.E.) and other civilizations.[4] We built the first universities. I am talking about the mystery schools of ancient Egypt (pre-3900 B.C.E.), the University of Sankore in Timbuktu (c. 1490 C.E.), and the great West African educational centers at Kumbi-Saleh, Djenna, and Gao (pre-1090 C.E.) among others.[5]

We were the first scientists: Imhotep (c. 2980 B.C.E.) who was also the Father of Medicine centuries before the Greek Hippocrates (460–370 B.C.E.), Hermes Trismegistus (c. 50 C.E.), the Egyptian founder of the arts and sciences, and Al-Jahiz (778–868 C.E.), an African Arab who was expert in anthropology and zoology and founder of Arab literature, to name only a few.[6]

We were the first architects and builders. For example, Zoser (c. 2980 B.C.E.), pharaoh of Egypt, builder of the stepped pyramid at Saqqara, the first builder to use hewn stone in architecture; Cheops, or Khufu (c. 2900 B.C.E.), pharaoh of Egypt, builder of the Great Pyramid at Gizeh; Chephren, or Khaf-Re (2861 B.C.E.), builder of the Second Pyramid at Gizeh; and Mycerinus, or Men-Kau-Re (2800 B.C.E.), pharaoh of Egypt, builder of the Third Pyramid at Gizeh.[7]

We were the first artists and musicians. There was Terence Afer (190–159 B.C.E.), playwright, poet, artist who delighted ancient Rome, and Ibn Soreyj (d. 724 C.E.), known as the first musician, an Arab black who introduced the flute to the people of Mecca.[8]

We were the first philosophers and mathematicians. There was Manetho (c. 304 B.C.E.), the Egyptian priest who composed

---

4. See Chancellor Williams, *The Destruction of Black Civilization: Great Issues of a Race from 4500 B.C. to 2000 A.D.* (Chicago: Third World Press, 1987), pp. 195–208.

5. See George G. M. James, *Stolen Legacy: Greek Philosophy Is Stolen Egyptian Philosophy* (New York: Philosophical Library, 1954; republished: African Publication Society, 1980; reprinted: Newport News, Va.: United Brothers Communications, 1989), pp. 131–137. See also Chancellor Williams, *The Destruction of Black Civilization*, p. 205.

6. See J. A. Rogers, *World's Great Men of Color*, vol. 1, with an introduction by John Henrik Clarke (New York: Collier Books-Macmillan Publishing Co., 1972), pp. 38–42, 163–171. On Hermes Trismegistus see *Saint Augustine: The City of God against the Pagans*, vol. 3, trans. David S. Wiesen, Loeb Classical Library Series (Cambridge: Harvard University Press, 1968), book 8.23, pp. 103–114.

7. See John G. Jackson, *Introduction to African Civilizations*, pp. 13, 98; see also J. A. Wilson, "Egypt," *The Interpreter's Dictionary of the Bible*, vol. 2 (Nashville: Abingdon Press, 1980), p. 44.

8. See J. A. Rogers, *World's Great Men of Color*, pp. 118–120, 162.

a philosophical and religious history of the Egyptians for Ptolemy I Soter (d. 283 B.C.E.), Macedonian conqueror of Egypt; and Ptolemy (Claudius Ptolemaeus) of Alexandria (c. 151 C.E.), an astronomer and mathematician who codified the teachings of the Alexandrian (African) scholars.[9]

We were the first navigators and explorers, like the mysterious Nubian-Egyptian mariners who encountered and interacted with the great Olmecs of Central Mexico (800–700 B.C.E.), and Abubakari II (c. 1311 C.E.), king of Mali, whose fleet voyaged to "the Americas" 181 years before Christopher Columbus.[10]

We were the first statesmen and diplomats, like Pharaoh Nectanebo I (c. 383 B.C.E.) Egyptian diplomat-soldier during the time of the Persian occupation of Egypt; Cleopatra VII (69–30 B.C.E.), queen of Egypt when Julius Caesar (100–44 B.C.E.) and his grandnephew Octavian (Augustus, 63 B.C.E.–14 C.E.) were casting an ominous shadow; and Ann Zingha (1582–1663 C.E.) diplomat and warrior-queen of Matamba, West Africa, during the time of Portuguese encroachment under King John IV (d. 1656 C.E.).[11]

We were the first teachers and poets, like Aesop (c. 560 B.C.E.), or Ethiop, the famed teller of fables and proverbs who inspired philosophers and sages of all cultures, and the numerous unnamed griots of precolonial West Africa.[12] We did not learn it from others, others learned it from us; and then they used it against us to turn us into slaves.

But it is still there — that spark — no, that fire of creativity is still there within us. Slavery has not put it out. Racism has not put it out. Miseducation has not put it out. It is still there. We see it in our music. We see it in our dance. We see it in our art. We see it in our scholarship. We see it in our technology. We see it in our

9. See John G. Jackson, *Introduction to African Civilizations*, p. 96. See also Herb Boyd, *African History for Beginners*, part 1: *African Dawn — A Diasporan View* (New York: Writers and Readers Publishing, 1991), p. 38.

10. See Ivan Van Sertima, *They Came before Columbus* (New York: Random House, 1976), pp. 37–70, 143–179.

11. See J. A. Rogers, *World's Great Men of Color*, pp. 121–130, 247–250. And also J. A. Rogers, *Sex and Race: Negro-Caucasian Mixing in All Ages and All Lands*, vol. 1: *The Old World* (St. Petersburg: Helga M. Rogers, 1952; reprint 1968), p. 51.

12. See J. A. Rogers, *World's Great Men of Color*, vol. 1, pp. 73–80.

worship. That fire of creativity is still there. We just need to fan the flames more. This is what we are trying to do right now.

There is no doubt that these are critical times for African American people. We appear to be a devastated people. All of our hard-won gains have been systematically and subtly taken away or forfeited via our own neglect. In many ways we are worse off than we have ever been. The racism that we thought we had overcome has come back in newer and more difficult forms. Once our bodies were held in bondage by the iron chains of slavery, now our minds are held in bondage by the subtle chains of miseducation and self-hate. It makes us wonder if there is an answer to our crisis.

Well, I come to say that there is an answer. That answer is to recover the image of God within us. We can begin by learning the truth about ourselves and our history. We can begin by taking back our own heritage and tradition. We can begin by proudly becoming black and African again. The more African we are, the more natural and spiritual we are. The more African we are, the more social we are. The more African we are, the more creative we are. The more African we are, the more we look like God.

If after all of this, some people still want to argue with you about what color God is, don't argue with them. Just tell them to read the Bible again. There it is in Ezekiel 1:27: the color of God! But if they still want to argue with you, just tell them something that they cannot argue with. Just tell them, "All right, since you refuse to accept what Ezekiel said about the color of God, let's just talk about *spiritual* color." For us, "spiritual color" is not the shade of our skin, but rather those qualities within. Furthermore, "spiritual color" is not the way God's complexion might appear in a vision, but it is those aspects of God's character and activity that we should try to emulate. So then, just talk about "spiritual color" and tell them: "Whatever color love is, that's the color of God; whatever color justice is, that's the color of God; whatever color peace is, that's the color of God; whatever color freedom is, that's the color of God; whatever color joy is, that's the color of God; whatever color healing is, that's the color of God; whatever color wholeness is, that's the color of God; whatever color salvation is, that's the color of God; whatever color power is, that's the color of God; whatever color truth is, that's the color of God." So then, regardless of who we are or where we come from, regardless of our own skin color or racial identity, we should strive to be God's (spiritual) color. Amen.

# The African Identity of Jesus

### Ezekiel 1:26-28 and Revelation 1:12-16

In the preceding sermon, I identified the divine person revealed in Ezekiel 1:26-28 with the divine person revealed in Daniel 7:9 and Revelation 1:12-16. This is a theological position rooted in my belief in the unity of the Bible's testimony to God's self-disclosure.

In the next sermon, I press the identification between the person revealed in Ezekiel 1:26-28 and Revelation 1:12-16 even further to make a christological statement. This is rooted in my belief that the Christ is "the exact imprint of God's very being" (Hebrews 1:3, NRSV; cf. "the express image of [God's] person" [KJV]). I will press matters even further by identifying the person revealed in Revelation 1:12-16 with Jesus of Nazareth. This is a serious application of the belief that "the Word became flesh and lived among us" (John 1:14, NRSV). Furthermore, I am convinced that there is a general consistency between the description of the glorified Lord in Revelation 1:12-16 and the apostolic memory of the historical Jesus.

These identifications may be too great a theological leap for some, but they are nevertheless consistent with the way some quarters of the early church read the Scriptures, and the way many contemporary African American churches and churches of other cultures still read the Scriptures.

In any case, a recorded vision of the Divine, such as Ezekiel 1:26-28 and Revelation 1:12-16, also reflects the human and social environment through which that vision is filtered. Therefore, a vision of God or Christ with typically African features, for example, would, at the very least, indicate a predominantly African milieu as the environmental matrix where that vision was conceived or received. The historical Jesus was, after all, a product of this kind of milieu. This then is another reason for maintaining that there is historical continuity and identity between the glorified Christ of Revelation 1:12-16 and Jesus of Nazareth.

W E HAVE SAID BEFORE that a people who do not know their past do not have a future.

This is Black History month, and it is during this month that we will join other churches and community groups in lifting up and celebrating the historical significance and contributions of black people, especially black people in America.

In most of our churches this month we will hear about such great black heroes and "she-roes" as Mary McLeod Bethune (1875–1955), a black woman who built a college on top of a garbage dump in Daytona, Florida.

We will hear about Benjamin Banneker (1731–1806), a black man who was also a scientist, mathematician, and astronomer, who was instrumental in the design and layout of Washington, D.C.

We will hear about George Washington Carver (1864?–1943), a black man and great agricultural chemist who developed hundreds of products from the peanut, soybean, and sweet potato.

We will hear about Sharon Pratt Kelly (elected 1990), a black woman, who at this very moment in history is the mayor of Washington, D.C.

We will hear about L. Douglas Wilder (elected 1990), a black man, who is at this very moment in history the governor of the State of Virginia.

We will hear about Maxine Waters (elected 1991), a black woman, who is the representative from California to the United States Congress.

We will hear about Tom Bradley (elected 1973), a black man, who is mayor of Los Angeles. We will hear about Kurt Schmoke (elected 1987), a black man, who is mayor of Baltimore, and we will hear about David N. Dinkins (elected 1990), a black man, who is mayor of New York City.

Yes, all over this country we will be talking this month about black men and black women, both past and present, who have and still are making contributions of great worth and great weight to the nation and the world. We will lift up and celebrate their contributions and achievements for the purpose of inspiring ourselves and our children with their examples of greatness. Certainly, this is good and much needed.

There is, however, one major problem with many of our black history celebrations (beside the fact that we tend to restrict them to only one month in the year), and this is a problem that I have noticed with many of the black history observances that I have been invited to participate in. That problem is this: when we rehearse our history, we tend to speak as if we had no history until we were brought to the Americas as slaves. We do not seem to realize that our history goes back further than Jamestown 1619, when we were first deposited upon these forboding shores as slaves. We do not seem to realize that our contributions and achievements are not limited to the nearly four hundred years we have spent in the Americas.

This is why when I speak of black history I not only like to go back, but I like to go w-a-ay back...w-a-ay, w-a-ay back... back two thousand to three thousand years to ancient history, back to biblical history.

Now don't get me wrong. We need to lift up and celebrate those notable black men and black women who are with us right here and right now. Yes, we need to recognize and acknowledge those outstanding black men and black women in more modern contexts who are at this very moment making history. And we need to lift up and celebrate those notable black men and women from our fathers' and mothers' time, and from our grandfathers' and grandmothers' time. Harriet Tubman, Sojourner Truth, Marcus Garvey, Malcolm X, Martin Luther King, Jr. — we must remember them all!

And then we need to go back — w-a-ay, w-a-ay back — just to demonstrate that we are not latecomers on the stage of history. And not only for that reason, but we must go back for the *truth's* sake. For the sake of the truth we must show that many of the most important people in history were black people. They were important not only in black history but in history, period. These people were so important in history that the world would not be the world that it is today if it were not for these people, who just happened to be black. By "black" I mean having an African bloodline with any combination or degree of discernible African features.

The great personalities of early church history were black. The early Christian martyrs Perpetua (d. March 7, 203 C.E.) and Feliciti (d. March 7, 203 C.E.) of the African city of Carthage were black. Saint Augustine (354–430 C.E.) of the African city of Hippo was black. Tertullian (160–225 C.E.) and Cyprian (d. 258 C.E.) of the African city of Carthage were black. Origen (c. 185–c. 254 C.E.) of the African country of Egypt was black. There are many others in early church history and the Bible whom I could cite, but when I really want to demonstrate the importance and significance of black people in history, I focus on the one person who was the most important and most significant person who has ever lived, and that is Jesus of Nazareth.

Now, some people think that when I say that Jesus of Nazareth was a black man that I am trying to stir up controversy or start something. No, I am not trying to stir up controversy or start anything, but I am trying to put an end to something. I am trying to put an end to and undo the great amount of damage that has been done to the hearts, minds, and souls of black people who have been taught all of our lives that everything good and everything right is white and everything not so good and everything not so right is black. You see, after we say that "everything good is white and everything bad is black," it is only one small, unconscious, psychological step to say, "And this goes for people too." Let us not fool ourselves, white society has done this in very subtle and sneaky ways.

I remember when I was eight years old, in third grade in an "integrated" school. I was coloring in my little coloring book, and I was coloring pictures of children. First of all, there were no black children depicted in my coloring book. This was bad enough. Second, as I was coloring the pictures of what were obviously little white boys and white girls in my coloring book, I noticed the name of the crayon that I was using. The reason I was using this particular crayon was because it was the appropriate color for the pictures of little white boys and white girls . . . you know, kind of whitish pink. But when I looked at the name of the crayon, I saw that the name was not "pink" or "whitish pink"; it was "flesh." The name of the crayon that I was using was "flesh." But when I looked at my flesh, it was clear to me that my flesh and that crayon were not the same color. In other words, that little crayon communicated a very powerful and very damaging message to me — and I know it affected me because I still remember this incident after all of these years. That message was that "the only flesh that really mattered, the only flesh that deserved recognition, the only flesh that merited having a crayon named after it, the only flesh that was truly worthy of being called flesh, was flesh that was *this* color." Suddenly, I was marginalized by a little crayon, and it is in very subtle and sneaky ways like this that negative messages are communicated to us about our identity.

But, oh, when I see Jesus . . . I see the opposite of everything that white society has ever tried to teach me about myself. When I see Jesus, I see the purest and the best that the world has ever known, and I also see a dark-skinned Palestinian Jew of African descent. I see a black man.

Yes, when I see Jesus, I see proof positive that to be black is still to be exceedingly good. I say this not to boast. I say this not to be arrogant. I say this so that my children and your children will know how good and wonderful they are. Despite what the world says to them and about them, they are wonderful. If there is a child sitting next to you, turn to that child right now and say to that child, "You are wonderful." Now, if there is a grown person sitting next to you, turn to that grown person and say to that person, "You are wonderful, too."

"Well, Pastor" somebody might ask, "how do you know that Jesus was a black man?" You know, it is interesting that nobody ever asks, "How do you know that Jesus was a white man?" It is only when we declare that he was black that we are called into question. But this is all right; we can still prove that Jesus was black.

First of all, we have the brief description of Jesus in Revelation 1:12-16 (the apocalyptic figure identifies himself as Jesus in Revelation 22:16). In that passage, the apostle John describes Jesus as having hair like snow white wool. It is interesting that when John the apostle describes Jesus' hair he evokes the image of lamb's wool. I believe that this is intentional. John not only wants to indicate the color of Jesus' hair, but also its texture. If Jesus' hair was long, flowing, and straight instead of short and curly then the image of lamb's wool just would not fit.

Furthermore, the apostle says that Jesus' feet were like "burnished bronze" refined in a fire (RSV), in other words, dark brown. It is understandable that John would describe Jesus' feet, because after he got a glimpse of Jesus' glory, he fell to Jesus' feet. His feet were all that he could look upon, and so when he recorded the Lord's appearance he remembered the color of Jesus' feet as well as the color and texture of Jesus' hair. It just doesn't make sense to say that the color of Jesus' feet was different from the rest of his body.

The apostle John's vision of Jesus reminds us of the vision of the prophet in Ezekiel 1:26-28. However, in this case, Ezekiel describes the Lord's upper body instead of his feet, and he says that the appearance of the Lord's upper body was as "gleaming bronze" (RSV). That is to say, the Lord was dark-skinned.

Second, we know that Jesus was black because he had black people in his family tree. In the very first chapter of the Gospel of Matthew, we learn that Jesus was descended from a woman named Tamar, a woman named Rahab, and a woman named Bathsheba, the widow of Uriah who became the wife of David the king. Tamar and Rahab were Canaanites, and Bathsheba was a Hittite (descendant of Heth). According to the tenth chapter of Genesis, the Canaanites and the Hittites were the descendants of Ham, and Ham was the father of all black African nations including the Egyptians and the Ethiopians. In fact, the very word "Ham" (*Chem* or *Khem*) is an Egyptian word that means "blackened by the sun" (or "heated" or "burnt"). Since Mary was also a descendant of David the king like her husband Joseph, she also had a manifest African bloodline. Therefore, the doctrine of the virgin birth does not exclude Jesus from an African bloodline. As a descendant of black people through his forefather David and his mother, Mary, Jesus was also black. He was a Jew of black African descent.[1]

---

1. See Rev. Walter Arthur McCray, *The Black Presence in the Bible: Discovering the Black and African Identity of Biblical Persons and Nations* (Chicago: Black Light Fellowship, 1990), pp. 125–129. See also Joachim Jeremias, *Jerusalem in the Time of Jesus* (Philadelphia: Fortress Press, 1981), p. 365 and also footnote 32. Jeremias points out that marriage between kin (i.e., people with the same bloodline) was a common practice in first-century Palestine.

Third, thanks to the research of the late scholars, Robert Eisler and Joel A. Rogers, we know about the testimony of Flavius Josephus (c. 37–c. 100 C.E.), that first-century historian of the Jewish nation, who said that Jesus was, among other things, a man of "simple appearance," "dark skin," and "little hair." Who other than this ancient witness and the apostles could speak with more authority about the appearance of Jesus?[2]

Finally, we know that Jesus was black because the earliest known paintings and portraits of Jesus and his mother showed them as black. If we travel to Germany, France, Italy, and other countries of Europe to the great museum churches and cathedrals and if we look in some of their back rooms, corridors, and closets where they have been hidden, we will find paintings and portraits of Black Madonnas and Christs that go way back in time. It was in the sixteenth century (1508–1512), when Pope Julius II (1443–1513) commissioned Michelangelo (1475–1564) to start painting when all of these depictions of a black Mary and black Jesus were replaced by depictions of a white Mary and white Jesus. This replacement, however, was the culmination of a tendency that actually began as early as the third or fourth centuries.[3] Michelangelo was followed by Leonardo da Vinci (1452–1519), Raphael (1483–1520), and others.[4] They were the ones responsible for "changing" Jesus from black to white; we must be responsible for "changing" Jesus back to black.[5]

---

2. J. A. Rogers, *Nature Knows No Color-Line: Research into the Negro Ancestry in the White Race* (St. Petersburg: Helga M. Rogers, 1952; reprint 1980), pp. 40–41. Robert Eisler, *The Messiah Jesus and John the Baptist according to Flavius Josephus' Recently Rediscovered "Capture of Jerusalem" and Other Jewish and Christian Sources* (London: Methuen, 1931), pp. 393, 420–421, 618–619. The extant Greek manuscript of Josephus's "On the Physical Appearance of Jesus" is preserved in the collection of Ernst v. Dobschütz, and appears on pp. 618–619 of Eisler's book. Its authenticity as the work of Flavius Josephus is attested by Andreas Hierosolymitanus (b. 660 C.E.), also known as Cretensis, archbishop of Crete (c. 700 C.E.), and also by Eisler himself after applying the techniques of textual criticism to other manuscripts that tried to alter the original.

3. For example, the Europeanized versions of Jesus in the mosaics of the churches of San Vitale, Ravenna (in North Central Italy), some of which are dated before 549 C.E.. See F. van der Meer, *Early Christian Art,* trans. Peter and Friedl Brown (Chicago: University of Chicago Press, 1959), pp. 127–145.

4. Even now Warner Sallman's (1892–1968) *Head of Christ* (painted in 1940) is experiencing a revival of popularity with little regard on the part of its patrons for its implicitly racist message, however unintentional that message may have been at first.

5. Joel A. Rogers cited a gold coin (dated 705 C.E.) that was displayed in the British

Well, someone will respond to all of this by saying, "Why even be bothered with the question of whether Jesus is black or white?" "Why should we even talk about it?" Because it is an important issue with implications for our lives, that's why.

Just look around and take note. Many of us in this sanctuary today are afraid to come to church at night in this part of the city. Why are we afraid? We are afraid of being attacked, that's why. Attacked by whom? White people? No, white people do not even live around here. We are afraid of being attacked by our own people.

As a people, we have been filled with so much self-hate, we have been robbed of so much self-esteem, and we have been deprived of so much self-respect that we have turned upon ourselves and have become our own worst enemies. Gang violence and drive-by shootings, drug trafficking and drug use, black-on-black crime and victimization are all symptoms of a self-hating people. They are symptoms of a people who have been taught and who have believed that nothing good has come out of Africa.

We must now turn our situation around, but before we can do that we must first turn our hearts and minds around. We can begin with the realization that Jesus of Nazareth, who was heaven's best sent down to dwell among us, was not the straight-haired blond, blue-eyed white European that we see portrayed on the walls and stained-glass windows of our churches, but rather, he was a black-skinned Palestinian Jew of African descent.

So then, when we mistreat one another, we are mistreating Jesus. When we hurt one another, we are hurting Jesus. When we tear down one another, we are tearing down Jesus. When we kill one another, we are killing Jesus. But, oh, on the other hand, when we love one another, we are loving Jesus. When we care for one another, we are caring for Jesus. When we help one another, we are

---

Museum. On one side was an engraved image of Justinian I (483–565 C.E.), who became emperor of the Byzantine (Eastern Roman) Empire in 527 C.E. On the other side was an engraved image of Jesus Christ. While the image of Justinian I was clearly "Caucasoid," the image of Jesus Christ was clearly "Negroid." A photograph of this coin along with commentary appears in J. A. Rogers, *Sex and Race: Negro-Caucasian Mixing in All Ages and All Lands*, vol. 1: *The Old World* (St. Petersburg: Helga M. Rogers, 1952; reprint 1968), pp. 81, 292. See also the comments in John L. Johnson, *The Black Biblical Heritage: Four Thousand Years of Black Biblical History* (Nashville: Winston-Derek Publishers, 1991), p. 236.

helping Jesus. "As you did it to one of the least of these ... you did it to me" (Matthew 25:40, RSV).

Yes, I know that it should not ultimately matter what color Jesus was. Regardless of whether Jesus was black, brown, red, yellow, or white, he would still be the Savior of the world and the Lord of all life, but black people have been lied to for so long and for intentionally destructive purposes that it is important to reveal the truth about the African identity of Jesus just for the sake of liberating our hearts and minds from generations of shame and self-hate.

We need to realize that we are well-represented in God's scheme of salvation. We are not just a footnote at the bottom of the script. We are not just scribble written in the margins of history. We are represented at the core of redemptive history. We are at the center of the salvation event.

And so I am saying to you: Don't let the world make you ashamed of who you are. Don't let the world force you to hate your African heritage and identity. Don't let the world cause you to despise the curliness of your hair, the darkness of your skin, the broadness of your nose, or the fullness of your lips. When God sent heaven's finest, he came as a little nappy-headed black boy growing up in the streets of Nazareth. He came looking like you and me. This means that what the world believes about us does not matter. It is who we are in the eyes of God that matters.

We can therefore face a hostile world with confidence and courage. Though the world despises us, God loves us. Though the world tears us down, God builds us up. Though the world holds us back, God brings us out. Though the world pushes us down, God lifts us up. Though the world locks us in, God sets us free. Though the world shuts us out, God takes us in. Though the world tells us "No," God tells us "Yes." Though the world takes from us, God adds to us. Though the world wounds us, God heals us. Though the world forsakes us, God stays with us. Though the world offends us, God defends us.

We, who are the children of Africa, have nothing to be ashamed of, for God loves and keeps us just as we are. Therefore, rather than be ashamed, we are thankful for God's love and we rejoice in God's power. Hallelujah! Thank you, Lord!

# We Need a Hero

### Acts 21:37-39

S OME OF YOU may have been watching the 1990 Grammy Awards last Wednesday night on television. For me, the most interesting aspect of this year's Grammy Awards was the announcement of the winner of the Song of the Year award. It was a winner whom I never would have guessed, and evidently, from the news reports, it was a surprise to a lot of other people who were supposedly "in the know." It was a song sung by Bette Midler, a nice little song entitled "The Wind Beneath My Wings." In this song, the singer is telling a special someone that he or she is the singer's hero and a model for the singer's life and aspirations. Thanks to this special someone, the singer is able to attain high levels of achievement, for this special someone is the singer's source of strength and encouragement.

Now, it is anybody's guess why this song won the Grammy Award for best song of the year. Some people will say that it was because Bette Midler sang it, and they may be right. Some will say that it was because the song has a catchy tune, and they may be right. But I think that there is another reason why this particular song won Song of the Year, and that is because people today really want heroes. We, in fact, need heroes. Whether we realize it or not, whether we acknowledge it or not, we probably need heroes now more than ever before.

I remember about a decade ago when Ronald Reagan came into

the office of the president of the United States and the American hostages in Iran were set free. Considerable debate erupted in this country when Ronald Reagan called the former hostages "heroes." Some people asked, "Why are we calling them heroes when all they did was survive?" One commentator observed, "It is because we are so desperate for heroes, that's why."

It was not too long after that when the United States National Aeronautics and Space Administration (NASA) launched the first space-shuttle mission. When the mission was completed, the media started calling the space-shuttle astronauts heroes. They did not rescue anyone. They went up, performed their duties, and then came back home. Yet they became heroes.

All of this illustrates that we have a desperate need for heroes, people to model ourselves after, people to look up to and admire.

One of the reasons that we as an African American people are celebrating African American history month is because we too have a desperate need for heroes. We need to have men and women of our own race that we can look up to and admire.

We have heroes like Lewis Latimer (1848–1928), who invented the carbon filament for Thomas Edison's (1847–1931) electric light bulb and who helped Alexander Graham Bell (1847–1922) perfect and patent his designs for the telephone.

We have heroes like Isabella Baumfree (1797–1883), also known as Sojourner Truth, who fought for the abolition of slavery and for women's rights.

We have heroes like Charles R. Drew (1904–1950), a surgeon who was responsible for saving thousands and thousands of lives as the one who pioneered the use of blood plasma in emergency blood transfusions and who established and directed the first American Red Cross blood bank.

We have heroes like Harriet Tubman (1826–1913), who was called "Black Moses," an abolitionist who risked her life as a conductor for the Underground Railroad.

We have heroes like Frederick Douglass (1817–1895), Wilma Rudolph (b. 1940), Bishop Richard Allen (1760–1831), Rosa Parks (b. 1913), Adam Clayton Powell (1908–1972), Gwendolyn Brooks (b. 1917), Paul Lawrence Dunbar (1872–1906), Constance

Baker Motley (b. 1921), and many, many others whom God has raised up as an example to us all. They are pastors, teachers, scientists, doctors, poets, lawyers, businessmen and businesswomen, athletes, artists, inventors, engineers, and politicians. They are heroes all, and we are thankful for them.

This morning, I want to go way back in time and talk about one of the great heroes of the Christian faith. This person whom I want to talk about is especially important for us during this black history observance because not only was he a follower of Jesus Christ, but he was a black man. He was a black man who made an immense contribution to both ancient and modern culture.

However, there is one problem with speaking about this person during Black History month, and that is that most people do not know that this person of whom I will speak was black. As a matter of fact, when I call his name, you will probably say to yourself, "I didn't know that he was black." Many of you will probably go away from this worship service this morning saying, "N-a-aw, he couldn't have been black. The preacher was off this morning. He couldn't have been black."

You know, in this modern age we have numerous advantages over people who lived in biblical and classical times, and two of them are photography and the video camera, two media that are vitally important today for recording and preserving history. I believe that if we today did not have the technology of photography and the video camera, several hundred years from now people would be saying that Martin Luther King, Jr., was white.

Furthermore, I become frightened when I turn on my television set and see white singers and singing groups who have learned how to imitate the sounds and moves of black singers and dancers. I wonder if people would be saying several hundred years from now that white people invented these sounds and moves and we learned it from them. I can almost hear them now, saying that white people invented jazz, gospel music, rhythm and blues, tap, rap, and break dancing and we, black folks, learned it from them. This is probably what they would say if not for the modern techniques of recording and preserving history (I am being humorous, of course).

Seriously though, you might think that this issue that I am raising is farfetched, and that I am way out in left field, and that I am being unfair, but this is not farfetched at all, and I am not being unfair. The truth of the matter is that what I am speaking of has already happened. It is already the case that blacks who have performed significant roles in the unfolding of history have been turned white and that the significant contributions and achievements of black people have been turned into white contributions and achievements.

We are about to see an example of this when I introduce the name of the biblical character whom I will be talking about today. Even though he was black, historians and artists have succeeded in turning him white. They have succeeded so well that when we mention his name, the vast majority of us will automatically picture him as a white man, when in actuality he was black. By "black" I mean having an African bloodline with any combination or degree of discernible African features.

Who was this great historical figure? Who was this great hero of the faith? Who was this black man? I'll tell you who he was. He was Paul the apostle, that's who.

"Paul the apostle!?"

"You mean, the same Paul the apostle who was knocked off his beast on the road to Damascus by a blinding light at noonday and then converted to faith in Jesus Christ?"

Yes, I mean that Paul the apostle.

"You mean, the same Paul the apostle who made three missionary journeys spreading the gospel and establishing churches throughout Asia and Europe?"

Yes, I mean that Paul the apostle.

"You mean, the same Paul the apostle who wrote thirteen of the twenty-seven books and epistles in the New Testament?"

Yes, I mean that Paul the apostle.

The revelation that I bring to you today is that Paul the apostle, one of the greatest heroes of the Christian faith, was a black man.

Well, I know that many of us are having difficulty believing this, so let us turn to the evidence in our Scripture text — Acts 21:37-39, where we have these words:

As Paul was about to be brought into the barracks, he said to the tribune, "May I say something to you?" And he said, "Do you know Greek? Are you not the Egyptian, then, who recently stirred up a revolt and led the four thousand men of the Assassins out into the wilderness?"

Paul replied, "I am a Jew, from Tarsus in Cilicia, a citizen of no mean city; I beg you, let me speak to the people." (RSV)

I would like for us to notice a couple of things in this often overlooked passage. First, we see that Paul the apostle was, at the time, under arrest for causing a disturbance. It was after he had completed his third missionary journey. Paul felt compelled to return to Jerusalem despite the warnings of his good friends. Paul wanted to share the good news of what God was doing among the Gentiles with his Jewish brothers and sisters in Jerusalem.

But Paul had many enemies in Jerusalem, and it was while he was visiting the temple in Jerusalem that his enemies saw him and then stirred up the crowd against him. Things became so much out of hand that a platoon of Roman soldiers had to come and rescue Paul by arresting him and taking him into custody.

If the life and experience of Paul the apostle show us anything, it is that it is not easy being a hero, especially a hero for Jesus Christ. Indeed, there are times when it will appear that a hero for Jesus Christ is no hero at all.

Being a hero for Jesus Christ means being an enemy to the world. Being a hero for Jesus Christ means, many times, having more people against us than for us.

But this is only for a while.

Being a hero for Jesus Christ also means that we will come out on top after all. Being a hero for Jesus Christ means that we will emerge from the battlefield victorious after all.

One of the fascinating aspects of the Nelson Mandela story in South Africa is how everything the South African government tried in order to stop the man only succeeded in making him even more powerful and more influential than ever.

They put him in jail for twenty-seven years, but instead of

making people forget him, this brought him even more into the arena of public attention.

They tried to discredit his anti-apartheid movement, but they only succeeded in making that movement an international cause.

They tried to demoralize his supporters, but they only succeeded in making them even more militant and determined.

This only shows that when God is behind a movement, that movement cannot be stopped. When God is behind a man or a woman, that man or woman cannot be stopped. When God is behind a revolution, that revolution cannot be stopped.

No, it is not easy being a hero for Jesus Christ, but that is all right, for the victory is guaranteed.

The second thing we should notice from this text in Acts 21:37-39 is that Paul was arrested not just for being the suspected cause of the commotion in Jerusalem but also because he was mistaken for an Egyptian who had earlier led a revolt against the Roman government.

Just read the text: While Paul was being taken to the prison barracks, he spoke to the officer who had him in custody, and when the officer heard Paul speaking to him in fluent Greek without an Egyptian accent, the officer began to realize that Paul may not be who his captors thought he was. So he asked Paul, "Are you not that Egyptian?"

The Bible does not tell us who this mysterious Egyptian was. He appeared to be an early Denmark Vesey (1767–1822), a Nat Turner (1800–1831), a Toussaint L'Ouverture (1744–1803), a Nelson Mandela who was opposing an oppressive Roman regime.[1] But still, the most interesting thing about this whole episode is that this Egyptian and Paul the apostle were thought for a while to be the same man. This is most interesting to us because if you have been listening to me over the course of the past few Sundays, you have heard me say that the ancient Egyptians like the ancient Ethiopians were not a white European or white Asian people as

---

1. See Josephus, *Jewish War* 2.13.5, and *Antiquities* 20.8.6. See also F. D. Gealey "The Egyptian," *The Interpreter's Dictionary of the Bible*, vol. 2 (Nashville: Abingdon Press, 1980), pp. 67–68.

some have tried to make us believe, but they were a North African black people who looked just like you and me.

The question this raises for us is, How could Paul the apostle be mistaken for a black African-Egyptian unless Paul himself looked like a black African-Egyptian? There was simply no way that anyone as widely traveled and as culturally and socially exposed as a Roman soldier could have mistaken a white man for an Egyptian. On the other hand, another black man of African descent could have very easily been mistaken for an Egyptian, especially if he did not say anything.

This reminds me of a time when I visited a conference on prayer and healing. That year the pianist for the conference was a highly talented and gifted young man from San Diego who was also a musician at a Pentecostal church. It just so happens that he and I have the same first names. Furthermore, we are about the same height and we are both black. He is a bit darker than I and a little heavier in build, but none of this helped much when it came to distinguishing us from one another. Even though I cannot play a lick, people who attended that conference still came up to me for as long as several months afterward to tell me how much they enjoyed my piano playing. You know what they say: We all look alike. In our text we also have a case of mistaken identity, and it could only have happened if Paul the apostle was also a man with black African features. Keep in mind that the Hebrews and their progeny, the Jews of first-century Palestine, were an Afroasiatic people. They were so African in appearance that, according to the Roman historian Tacitus, many people thought that the Jews were originally members of the Ethiopian race![2] No wonder Paul was mistaken for an Egyptian, a member of another African people.

Why am I pointing this out today? First of all, because it is

---

2. *History* 5.2, *The Complete Works of Tacitus,* trans. John Church and William Jackson Brodribb (New York: Random House, 1942), pp. 657–658. See also John L. Johnson, *The Black Biblical Heritage: Four Thousand Years of Black Biblical History* (Nashville: Winston-Derek Publishers, 1991), p. 55. An interesting aside: the city of Tarsus (in South Turkey), birthplace of Paul the apostle and possibly the world's oldest city in continuous existence, was reportedly founded by a wealthy Ethiopian nobleman named Sandan (Ammianus Marcellinus, *Constantius et Gallus* 14.8.3, *Ammianus Marcellinus,* vol. 2, trans. John C. Rolfe, Loeb Classical Library Series (Cambridge: Harvard University Press, 1950), p. 67.

the truth, and it is time to overthrow the falsehood that the greatest personalities of history were all white Europeans or persons of white European descent. Second, I am pointing this out because our children need heroes, and we also need heroes, heroes we can admire, heroes who will inspire. And we do not have to look far to find them. Right here in the Bible — the greatest book of black history there ever was, we have an abundance of heroes to choose from.

- Moses (1350?-1230? B.C.E.), the deliverer of the Hebrews was a black man.

- David (1000–962 B.C.E.) and Solomon (c. 972–932 B.C.E.), the greatest kings that Israel ever had, were black men.

- The queen of Sheba (c. 960), the wealthiest and most powerful woman in the world, was a black woman.

- Simon of Cyrene (7 B.C.E.?–43 C.E.?), who helped Jesus carry the cross, was a black man.

- Mary of Nazareth (23 B.C.E.?–38 C.E.?), the mother of Jesus, was a black woman.

- Jesus of Nazareth (4 B.C.E.?–29 C.E.), who had hair like lamb's wool and skin like burnished bronze, was a black man.

- And Paul, the great apostle to the nations, was a black man.

So then, if it is heroes that we need, we can start right here with this Bible. We have them . . . right here in this book:

- Heroes who knew how to hold on to God's unchanging hand,

- Heroes who knew how to face the storm and the rain,

- Heroes who stood steadfast on the promises of God,

- Heroes who did not let anybody turn them around,

- Heroes who were strong in the grace of God,

- Heroes who put on the whole armor of God,

- Heroes who did not get weary in well-doing,

- Heroes who fought the good fight,
- Heroes who finished their course,
- Heroes who kept the faith,
- Heroes who obtained their crown,
- Heroes who pressed toward the mark,
- Heroes who overcame the world.

God is still raising up heroes today. God is still raising up Christian men and women, young and old, who will be heroes to this generation.

If we would keep the faith, as Paul the apostle did, and run with patience the race that is set before us, then one day, someone somewhere will be able to look at any one of us and say that you and I are heroes, models for that someone's life and aspirations, inspirations for that someone to reach a high level of achievement, and sources for their strength and encouragement.

# We Were There

### Romans 16:13 and Mark 15:21

I N OUR SCRIPTURE TEXT, we have a very fleeting reference to
a rather obscure person named Rufus, whom Paul the apostle
describes as "eminent in the Lord," and to the mother of Rufus who
is evidently so dear to the apostle that he has adopted her as his own
mother. Obviously, Rufus and his mother were very important to
Paul, but it is also apparent that they were rather prominent and
influential in the church that gathered in Rome.

Who, then, are these obscure but influential Christian leaders, this mother and son, whom Paul the apostle felt obliged to
acknowledge with highest esteem in his great epistle to the congregation in Rome? For the answer we will have to travel back
in time approximately twenty-three years from the time the letter
to the Romans was written (56 C.E.) to an event that is recorded
in the Gospel of Mark (15:21). Here in this Gospel, the evangelist John Mark records the events leading up to the crucifixion of
Jesus of Nazareth. Near the end, the Roman soldiers force Jesus
to carry his own cross up the rugged road to Golgotha's hill. Jesus
has been brutally beaten. His physical energies are depleted. His
great stamina and strength have been exhausted. As he struggles
to bear up his cross, his arms and his legs give way and he falls
with the heavy wooden beam crashing down on top of him. The
mean-spirited Roman soldiers become impatient, yet they do not
want Jesus to die of exhaustion before they have fastened him to
the cross.

So according to Mark 15:21 they compelled a passerby, a North African black man by the name of Simon of Cyrene, to carry the cross of Jesus. We do not know much about Simon of Cyrene, but he is identified to the readers of Mark's Gospel as the father of Alexander and *Rufus*. This is the only place in the Synoptic Gospels where Simon of Cyrene is identified as the father of Alexander and Rufus. It demonstrates for us that Alexander and Rufus were well-known and prominent individuals in the early Christian community. They were especially well known in the Christian community that John Mark belonged to and wrote for, namely, the congregation in Rome.[1] Therefore, in Mark's Gospel we learn the identities of this eminent Christian leader and his mother who are mentioned in the last chapter of Romans. He is the son of Simon of Cyrene. His mother, of course, is the wife of Simon of Cyrene.[2] Rufus is probably the younger of the two since Mark mentions him after Alexander. Simon of Cyrene is not mentioned in Paul's Epistle to the Romans; neither is Alexander. It could be that by this time they have both gone home to be with the Lord. We cannot say with certainty. It appears, however, that the wife of Simon was a widow now and was being cared for by Rufus, who was her only remaining son.

The presence of Rufus and his mother in the Roman Christian church is highly significant for us who are African American, for their presence is more evidence of the prominence and influence of African black people in the early Christian church.

I have said it before; I will say it again. We were there from the very beginning of Christianity. Black people were there! For too many times the falsehood has been propagated that we would have known nothing of the Christian faith if not for the European slave traders and their American patrons who brought us to the

---

1. *Eusebius: The Ecclesiastical History*, trans. Kirsopp Lake, Loeb Classical Library Series (Cambridge: Harvard University Press, 1953), vol. 2, 16.1–2; 17.1–2, p. 145. See also Lamin Sanneh, *West African Christianity: The Religious Impact* (Maryknoll, N.Y.: Orbis Books, 1983), pp. 2–3.

2. Interestingly, St. Epiphanius (c. 310–320 C.E.), bishop of Salamis (an island East of Greece in the Gulf of Aegina), speaks of "Mary the mother of Rufus" who stood at the cross with the other women disciples and witnessed the crucifixion of Jesus (*Antidicomarianites* 13.2, *The Panarion of St. Epiphanius, Bishop of Salamis*, trans. Philip R. Amidon [New York: Oxford University Press, 1990], p. 349).

Americas in chains and eventually got around to turning us into Christians. Nothing could be further from the truth. Simon of Cyrene, Simon of Cyrene's wife, Alexander bar-Simon, and Rufus bar-Simon were there at the very beginnings of Christianity. They were Christians and they were black.

Not only do we know about the family of Simon of Cyrene, particularly Rufus and his mother, but we know about other early Christian black people. In the book of Acts (13:1), we learn about five men in the city of Antioch (c. 50 C.E.) who are identified as Christian prophets and teachers. We can be sure that at least three of these men were black men. The first was Simeon Niger, whose last name actually means "the black man"; the second was Lucius of Cyrene, the same black African country that the father of Rufus was from; the third was Saul, also known as Paul the apostle, who was so African in his appearance that he was mistaken for an Egyptian in Acts 21:38.

Furthermore, if we back up to the second chapter of Acts, to the day of Pentecost when the Holy Spirit came and three thousand people were converted to faith in Jesus Christ all at one time, we will discover that there were black people there, representing at least three black African countries, namely, Egypt, Cyrene, and Libya, not to omit the Asiatic countries of Mesopotamia and Elam, which were also populated by black-skinned people of African descent.

Further still, in Acts 8 we read about the apostle Philip's encounter with a high-ranking official from the black African country of Ethiopia (tradition names him Judich).[3] Philip is commanded by an angel of the Lord to go up to this man and share with him the gospel of Jesus Christ (Acts 8:26-29). This man becomes the first Jewish proselyte to be converted to Jesus Christ after the

---

3. Lamin Sanneh, *West African Christianity*, p. 3. Sanneh says that Judich is named by Eusebius. However, more specific information may be needed. In Eusebius, *Ecclesiastical History* 2.10–14 and other relevant and related sections, a name for the Ethiopian eunuch does not appear. See, for example, *Eusebius: The Ecclesiastical History*, trans. Kirsopp Lake, Loeb Classical Library Series (Cambridge: Harvard University Press, 1953), vol. 1, pp. 107–111. According to G. T. Stokes, *The Acts of the Apostles* (New York: A. C. Armstrong and Son, 1903), p. 415, the name "Indich" or "Indictus" is given to the Ethiopian eunuch by Ethiopian tradition.

day of Pentecost. He was an Ethiopian black man, and he took his newfound faith back home with him.[4]

Many people believe that the black church did not come into being until the time of slavery in America. The truth is that the black church existed in Africa centuries before Christianity reached the Angles and the Saxons in Europe.[5] As a matter of fact, black people were among the founders of the oldest Christian church in the world, the Coptic Church of Egypt.[6]

We know that Christianity was planted in Egypt by the evangelist John Mark, former companion of Paul the apostle and Barnabas, but who was, at the time, bishop of Alexandria.[7] This led to the founding of the Coptic Church of Egypt about thirty years after the Ascension of Jesus.[8] By the fourth century (327 C.E.) Coptic Christianity was transplanted to Ethiopia, resulting in the founding of another black church, the Ethiopian Orthodox Church.[9]

Indeed, the great third- and fourth-century architects of Christian thought and theology were North African black people. Saint Augustine of Hippo (354–430 C.E.), Tertullian of Carthage (c. 160–225 C.E.), Cyprian of Carthage (d. 258 C.E.), Origen of Egypt (185–254 C.E.), and Clement of Alexandria (150–215 C.E.) were the giants of Christian doctrine and leadership in the developing church, and they were black.[10]

All I am trying to say is that we were there! From the very beginnings of Christian faith we were there!

Furthermore, even if it were not for the European invasion of Africa and the introduction of white colonial "Christianity," even if it were not for the African enslavement in America and

---

4. See C. Eric Lincoln, *Race, Religion, and the Continuing American Dilemma* (New York: Hill and Wang, 1984), p. 253.

5. Ibid.

6. See Lamin Sanneh, *West African Christianity*, pp. 4, 6–8.

7. (St. Epiphanius, *Alogoi* 51.6.10, *The Panarion of St. Epiphanius*, p. 178.

8. See Lamin Sanneh, *West African Christianity*, p. 4.

9. See C. Eric Lincoln, *Race, Religion, and the Continuing American Dilemma*, p. 253; Lamin Sanneh, *West African Christianity*, p. xvii, 8, 243.

10. See C. Eric Lincoln, *Race, Religion, and the Continuing American Dilemma*, p. 25; Lamin Sanneh, *West African Christianity*, pp. 1–13; see also Yosef A. A. ben-Jochannan, *African Origins of the Major "Western Religions"* (Baltimore: Black Classic Press, 1991), pp. 73, 86, 100, 209.

the introduction to the slavemaster's "religion," Christianity would have *still* reached the African West Coast, naturally, without the "help" of white people, and it would have spread like wildfire, just as it is doing today in Africa.[11] We did not need white people to find Jesus. We did not need slavery to find Jesus. Jesus was already on his way![12]

All that I am saying is that black people were not latecomers to the Christian faith. We were not afterthoughts in God's plan of salvation, and we are not indebted to white people in Europe and America for the great heritage of the Christian faith. No, if there is any indebtedness, then it is the debt that we all owe to our African forebears.

I know that this goes against everything that we have been taught about early church history, but the truth must finally be known. When the seeds of Christianity began to sprout and became a great tree extending its branches throughout the world, we were there at every point in the process even from the beginning. Rufus, the son of Simon, and his mother are among the great host of witnesses to this truth.

It may be that Rufus and his brother were probably around eleven and twelve years old when their father Simon embarked upon his pilgrimage from Cyrene, North Africa, to Jerusalem. He was going to Jerusalem to celebrate the Passover, because he was a faithful Jew. Whether or not he had his wife and children with him, we do not know; but I am inclined to believe that Simon was committed to providing spiritual leadership and religious training for his family. This is important, especially for black families. The strongest and most stable families we have are those families where the man's role is instrumental in providing spiritual and religious guidance for his family. Don't get me wrong. It is also vitally

---

11. See Lamin Sanneh, *West African Christianity,* pp. 20–22, 168–169. As it turned out "Christianity" was introduced to the African West Coast by the Portuguese in 1482. By 1892, however, forms of West African Christianity would be redeemed from their European colonial encumbrances and allowed to find more natural, indigenous forms of expression.

12. The late Alex Haley may have alluded to this in his literary masterpiece *Roots* (Garden City, N.Y.: Doubleday and Co., 1976), pp. 104–105, where he speaks of the visit of "the moros" (itinerant African philosophers).

important for the woman of the house to be a woman of faith who also provides spiritual and religious leadership. In fact, many of our strong and stable families are led by women of faith, without the help of a man. Both women and men agree that our families are at their strongest and most stable when the husband and father is at least one of the family's spiritual and religious leaders. When both the man of the house and the woman of the house are people of faith, then we have an unbeatable combination.

Simon was therefore in Jerusalem on a pilgrimage. In this regard he was not special. Hundreds of thousands came from all over the Mediterranean world to participate in the Passover feast in Jerusalem. This Passover experience was destined to be special for Simon, for when he arrived in Jerusalem, he would soon cross paths with a humble carpenter named Jesus of Nazareth. Not only would this encounter change the life of Simon of Cyrene, but it would also change the lives of his family, especially the lives of his sons, Rufus and Alexander.

On everyone's pilgrimage through life there is a crossroads. Present at that crossroads is Jesus of Nazareth. What happens at that crossroads is up to each one of us, but we can rest assured that Jesus will cross the path of each of us, and when he does, we each will have an opportunity to change our lives.

As I meditate upon the story, I can envision with my mind's eye Simon of Cyrene, sitting like an African griot or storyteller, with his sons, Rufus and Alexander, other family members, and friends gathered around him, to tell the story of how he met Jesus on the path to Golgotha's hill. With the ears of my heart I can hear him telling them of how he was deeply moved at the very sight of the man struggling to carry his cross to the site of his own execution. I can hear him telling them about the anguish he felt in his soul when he saw Jesus collapse beneath the weight of this cross. If you would indulge my imagination, I can see his sons, Rufus and Alexander, perking up their ears as their father speaks of how the Roman soldiers forced him to carry the cross of this wounded man. But when Simon took up the cross, he felt something come over him, some power from above, the Holy Spirit, giving him strength that he did not know that he had. At the same time the eyes of Jesus and

Simon meet. No words are spoken, but something passes between them, and Simon knows that Jesus is grateful for his help. In that moment, with the cross of Christ upon his shoulders, Simon was seized by faith and made his decision to become a follower of Jesus Christ.

There will always be a cross. We cannot escape it. When your health takes a turn for the worse, remember, there will always be a cross. When a financial crisis occurs in your life, remember, there will always be a cross. When your marriage falls apart, remember, there will always be a cross. When your children disappoint you, remember, there will always be a cross. When things go bad on the job, remember, there will always be a cross. When you suffer from an error in judgment, remember, there will always be a cross. But the question is, Will we allow our cross to become an opportunity for faith or an occasion for despair? I am convinced that Simon of Cyrene allowed the cross he bore to become an opportunity for faith. It was this faith that he communicated to his sons.

If you would indulge my imagination further, I see Rufus, some years later, a young man who has grown up in the Christian community. Perhaps by this time his father has passed from the scene, and also his brother Alexander, leaving Rufus alone with his mother. By some series of circumstances they end up in Rome, where Rufus becomes a well-known and eminent member of the Roman church and his mother a highly respected saint. I can see them both, present in the church, each of them beaming with a humble, bittersweet pride every Easter or whenever the story is told of how a man named Simon of Cyrene one day carried the cross of Jesus up to Calvary. I can see John Mark, a fellow church member and historian of the gospel, sitting off to the side jotting down notes to himself, making sure that when he wrote his Gospel that the story of Simon of Cyrene, the father of Alexander and Rufus, would be remembered.[13]

Thank God, somebody always remembers! As black people we have been in constant danger of forgetting who we are and where we come from, not because we are a naturally forgetful people,

---

13. *Eusebius: The Ecclesiastical History*, 2.15, 6.14, p. 145.

but because those who oppress us have tried to cripple and control us by erasing from us our culture and identity. They have tried to rob us of our history, rob us of our heritage, rob us of our story, and rob us of our memory. They have even gone so far as to try to erase *us* from the pages of history. Book after book has been written and published without a single paragraph devoted to the role of African peoples in world history and civilization. Yet despite all of this, somebody always remembers! ... somebody always remembers! ... who we are and where we come from. Somebody always remembers what we have done and the contributions we have made. And now, even here, even in the Scriptures, even before the effort began to erase us from history, a Gospel writer named John Mark remembered that a black man named Simon of Cyrene helped carry the cross of Jesus up the rugged hill.

One thing that we as black people know a whole lot about is bearing crosses. We have been bearing crosses for centuries. Through the monstrous evils of slavery, we bore our cross. Through the trauma of Civil War, we bore our cross. Through the disappointment of Reconstruction, we bore our cross. Through the insult of Jim Crowism, we bore our cross. Through the terror of the Ku Klux Klan, we bore our cross. Through the struggles for civil rights, we bore our cross. Through the hypocrisy of modern-day politics, we are still bearing our cross.

But there is an answer to the cross, and that answer is the victory that Jesus Christ gives — victory over the cross, victory over oppression, victory over injustice, victory over death, victory over the grave, victory over the lie, victory over the Evil One. Though we be like Simon, forced to carry crosses that are painful to bear, Jesus gives us strength and power to persevere.

And so, just like Jesus, we will someday rise. Just like Jesus, we will someday overcome. Just like Jesus, we will someday win.

If we bear the cross, we will wear the crown.

If we walk to Golgotha, we will rise to glory.

If we endure the suffering, we will enter salvation.

We have been there from the beginning of God's plan of salvation; surely we will be there at the end. Hallelujah. Amen.

# The Beauty of Blackness
## The Song of Solomon 1:5

I N THIS MESSAGE, we will deal briefly with a number of questions. One of those will be, Why have we translated our Scripture text with the words "I am black *and* beautiful" rather than "I am black *but* beautiful"? There are very good reasons why we are using this former translation rather than the translation that you may have in your own Bibles, and we will get to those reasons. But first let us deal with some more preliminary questions like, Who is our speaker in today's Scripture text? Who is this so boldly and confidently proclaiming to us that she is black and beautiful? Well, first of all, we know from reading the eight chapters of the Song of Solomon that the speaker in our text may rightfully be called the bride of Solomon.

We know, of course, that Solomon, the third king of Israel, the son of the great King David, was the wisest man in the world, but our focus today is upon his bride, who describes herself as black and beautiful. She says, "I am black and beautiful, O daughters of Jerusalem, like the tents of Kedar, like the curtains of Solomon" (NRSV). Not only does she say that she is black, but she goes on to tell us just how black she is. She is as black as the tents of Kedar. Kedar is the name of a north Arabian bedouin people who were in the habit of making their tents out of goat hair. The particular goats that were indigenous to that region were extremely black. Therefore, the bride of Solomon is saying to us that she is not merely suntanned, but black, deep black.

You see, even though the majority of people in the Old Testament world were either black African people or Asians of black African heritage (Afroasiatics), there were still some people who were blacker than others. For example, while the bride of Solomon describes herself as "black as the tents of Kedar," she describes her lover, Solomon, as "ruddy" in color (Song of Solomon 5:10, NRSV). Incidentally, in 1 Samuel 16:12 and 17:42, David, the father of Solomon, is also described as "ruddy" in color. Now through the years, we have been told, mainly by white Bible scholars, that the word "ruddy" only means "suntanned." But when we research the word, which is *edom* in Hebrew, we discover that the word does not mean "suntanned" but "reddish-brown." There are some of us in this sanctuary who could be called "ruddy" in the Old Testament sense. There are others of us in this sanctuary just a little bit too dark to be called "ruddy." We are a rainbow of blackness. But this is all right; according to the bride of Solomon, she is black and beautiful, and according to 1 Samuel 16:12, David is "ruddy, and . . . handsome (NRSV)." From a biblical perspective, no matter what shade of black you are, you are beautiful.

When I was in South Africa several months ago, I saw black people of all shades and hues, from caramel brown to charcoal black. As a matter of fact, when I saw one African brother I had to do a double take, because this brother was the blackest black that I have ever seen. You know, most of us in this room are not really black, but brown. But this brother that I saw was as black as coal. He was so black that seeing him made me feel white. I thought about this brother when I studied the words of the bride of Solomon. She just wants us to know that she is as black as they come, *and* she is beautiful.

So we know that the beautiful black woman of our text is the bride of Solomon, but that is not all that we know about her. We also know more specifically who she is. "Well, who is she then, Pastor?" She is the queen of Sheba, the wealthiest, most powerful, and most revered woman in the Mediterranean world. We first meet her in 1 Kings 10:1-13.[1] In this passage, the queen of Sheba comes to visit Solomon the king because she heard about his wisdom and his faith. She came to test his wisdom, but we know from other ancient sources that she ended up being swept off her feet and falling in love with the man, and the feeling was mutual. We do not know what love is until we read about the love between this black man and this black woman in the eight chapters of the book of the Song of Solomon. This book is so steamy that it almost did not make it into the Bible. It is so hot that the early Christian saints tried to "fix" it. They said, "Well, no, this book is not really about the love between a man and a woman, but about the love between Jesus Christ and his church." Yeah, sure, all right, we'll go along with that, but the rock-bottom truth is that this book is also about the love between a man and a woman, and not just between a man and a woman, but between a black man and a black woman. Does this shock you? There is more.

Not only do we know that the beautiful black woman in our text is the bride of Solomon, not only do we know that she is the queen of Sheba, but we also know her name. It is not from the Bible that we know her name, but from other historical sources.[2] What is her name, then? Her name is Makeda. She was an Ethiopian woman who became queen of the country of Sheba around the year 960 B.C.E. We know the country of Sheba, or at least a portion of it, by a different name now. That country is very much in today's news. The country of Sheba is today called Saudi Arabia (or Yemen). It is fascinating that in the Gospel of Matthew (12:42; cf. Luke 11:31) we have Jesus saying that "the queen of the South will arise at the judgement with this generation and condemn it; for she came from the ends of the earth to hear the wisdom of Solomon, and behold, something greater than Solomon is here" (RSV). We

---

1. See J. A. Rogers, *World's Great Men of Color*, vol. 1 (New York: Collier Books-Macmillan Publishing Co., 1972), pp. 81–88.

2. See J. A. Rogers, *World's Great Men of Color*, p. 81. See also John G. Jackson, *Introduction to African Civilizations*, with an introduction by John Henrik Clarke (Secaucus, N.J.: Citadel Press, 1970), p. 268. Rogers and Jackson identify the chief source as *The Kebra Nagast* (Glories of the Kings of Ethiopia), a collection of Ethiopian manuscripts dating back to the fourteenth century C.E.. Jackson says that an English translation of the manuscripts was published by Sir E. A. Wallis Budge (London: Oxford University Press, 1923).

know that when Jesus speaks of "the queen of the South" that he is speaking about the queen of Sheba. What many of us do not realize is that Jesus is also speaking of a black woman named Makeda, the same woman who said, "I am black and beautiful."

"But waitaminute, Pastor! I am having a problem here. My Bible translation does not say, "I am black *and* beautiful." My translation says, "I am black *but* beautiful." Yes, it is as if to be black and beautiful is an exception to the rule. People easily accept being white and beautiful, but to be black and beautiful is a shock and a surprise. So then, some translations of the text read as if the bride of Solomon is saying, "Yeah, I am black, but I am not ugly like other blacks are. I am an exception. I am beautiful." It is this type of deeply submerged message that we must eliminate from our consciousness. We must begin to see that to be black *is* to be beautiful.

The other day I was in a Christian bookstore getting some materials when it occurred to me that since I was planning to preach this message that I should go to the Bible shelf and compare the different translations of the Song of Solomon 1:5. What I found was interesting. The King James Version translates the sentence: "I *am* black, *but* comely." The New English Bible translates it: "I am dark *but* lovely." The Living Bible says: "I am dark *but* beautiful." The Revised Standard Version says: "I am very dark, *but* comely." The New American Standard Bible says: "I am black *but* lovely." The New International Version reads: "Dark I am, *yet* lovely." Then I came to a translation called the Easy-to-Read Version, and it said: "I am dark *and* beautiful." Then I looked in the Anchor Bible Commentary and it said: "Black I am *and* beautiful."[3] Finally, I came to the New Revised Standard Version of the Bible, the newest translation on the market, and it said: "I am black *and* beautiful" (all of the above, author's emphasis). In other words, I looked at nine translations of the biblical text. Six of them said essentially, "I am black *but* beautiful," and three of them said essentially, "I am black *and* beautiful."

---

3. Marvin H. Pope, *Song of Songs: A New Translation with Introduction and Commentary* (New York: Doubleday and Co., 1977), p. 1.

You see, here is the problem: the Song of Solomon, like most of the Old Testament, was originally written in Hebrew. The Hebrew phrase *she-tu-rah a-ni we-na-rah* can be translated either of two ways, either "I am black *but* beautiful" or "I am black *and* beautiful." Even though I found only three out of the nine translations that support the rendering "I am black *and* beautiful," I am convinced that these three translations are the correct ones. You see, black people in the ancient and biblical world would not have experienced the type of racism that we experience today. They would not have learned the lessons of self-hate, nor would they have developed a negative perspective upon their own blackness. They would not apologize for being black, nor would they think that there was an inconsistency between being black and beautiful. A black woman in the ancient or biblical world was therefore more likely to say, "I am black *and* beautiful" than "I am black *but* beautiful."

This is important to realize. Down through the years we have been carefully and systematically trained to see our blackness or our Africanness as evil and negative. We have been taught to hate everything about ourselves because we were not white. For example, just listen to how custom, the media, and the English language itself teaches us to despise the very idea of blackness:

- When Hollywood actors or performers are shunned or ostracized for taking a controversial stand, they are said to be "blacklisted."

- When children grow up to become bitter disappointments to their families, they are called the "black sheep" of their families.

- A person who is found guilty of the crime of extortion is called a "blackmailer."

- Hypocritically to accuse someone of being wrong when the accuser is equally wrong is described as "the pot calling the kettle black."

- People usually refer to the worst day of their lives as "the blackest day" of their lives.

- The political candidate who is expected to lose an election is many times referred to as "the dark horse" in a political campaign.

- On Monday, October 19, 1987, the stock market took a nose-dive causing a lot of people to lose a lot of money. That tragic day became known as "Black Monday."

- In the old-time cowboy movies, the good guys wore white hats, the bad guys wore black hats.

- If a sorority or fraternity conspired to keep you from joining its membership, the word would get out that you were being "blackballed."

- An acceptable and forgivable lie is called a "white lie," but the worst lie anyone can tell is a "black lie."

- If you go to the bakery and ask for an angel food cake, the baker will give you a white cake; if you ask for a devil's food cake, the baker will give you a black cake.[4]

Society itself instills within us a negative perspective on everything black. It is only a small, unconscious psychological step to transfer all of this negative feeling to black people — even among ourselves. Some of us have responded to this by trying to become as white as we can in terms of our values and our behavior. Others of us have responded by embarking upon a course of self-destruction. But it is time to overthrow this legacy of self-hate. It is time to free our minds of this brainwashing. It is time for us to realize that black is beautiful and that we are beautiful.

Just for the record, I want to point out that Makeda, the bride of Solomon and Jesus' queen of the South (Matthew 12:42; Luke 11:31), was not the only black woman in the Bible. No, Eve, the mother of all humanity, was a black woman. Hagar, the Egyptian handmaiden of Sarah and the mother of the Ishmaelites (the Arabs), was a black woman. Sarah, the wife of Abraham and the

---

4. Based on a sermon by the Reverend Zan W. Holmes, Jr., at the North Texas Annual Conference of the United Methodist Church, in which he addressed the issue of racism in the English language.

mother of the Israelites, was a black woman. Miriam, the sister of Moses and Aaron, was a black woman. Zipporah, the wife of Moses, was a black woman. Deborah, the judge of Israel, was a black woman. Tamar, the daughter-in-law of Judah, was a black woman. Rahab, the Canaanite who helped the Hebrew spies in Jericho, was a black woman. Bathsheba, who became the wife of David the King, was a black woman. The Candace, queen of Ethiopia in the book of Acts (8:27), was a black woman. Mary of Nazareth, the mother of Jesus, was a black woman.

Yes, when we look at biblical history, we discover that the sisters were there! When life had its first beginnings, the sisters were there! When the covenants between God and humanity were established, the sisters were there! When God delivered the people from bondage in Egypt, the sisters were there! When God turned back the enemies of Israel, the sisters were there! When God's plan of salvation was revealed through the prophets, the sisters were there! When the Word of God became flesh, the sisters were there! When the gospel mission expanded to the ends of the earth, the sisters were there!

We can go even further. There were some great black women of ancient history that we know about whose names are not found in our Bibles. There was Hatsheput, queen of Egypt (c. 1500 B.C.E.), a black woman who was the first woman in all of history to rule a nation. There was Nefertiti, the queen of Egypt (c. 1375 B.C.E.), a black woman who lived about four centuries before the queen of Sheba, who was renowned as the world's most beautiful woman. She and her husband, the pharaoh Akhenaton, a black man, were the first to teach that there is only one God. We also know about Nefertari II the Nubian (1292–1225 B.C.E.), a black woman who became queen of Egypt when she married the pharaoh Rameses II, whom Moses told, "Let my people go." And then there was Cleopatra VII (69–30 B.C.E.), the queen of Egypt, a black woman, one of the world's greatest diplomats and rulers. She even had Julius Caesar, Mark Anthony, and the whole Roman empire wrapped around her little finger.

They were black! They were beautiful! They were powerful! The queen of Sheba was not the only one. She stood in good company. And we stand in good company also ... if we will keep the faith ... if we will run the race ... if we will fight the good fight ... if we will hold up the banner of the Lord and not let anything turn us around. We stand in good company if we would love ourselves the way God made us. We stand in good company if we remember who we are and whose we are. We stand in good company — the company of overcomers.

As I conclude, I just want us to realize that our history as a people does not begin on a slave auction block in the antebellum American South; furthermore, our history does not begin with the European invasion of Africa; no, our history stretches way back, back to the great kings and queens of Africa, back to the great civilizations and cultures of Egypt and Ethiopia, Mali, Songhay, Ghana, and the Mossi states. We come from a great people. We come from great nations.

Why am I lifting these things up today? Because we must know the truth, that is why. In order to regain our self-respect and self-esteem, we must know the truth. In order to recover our sense of pride, we must know the truth. In order to save our boys and girls, we must know the truth. In order to rebuild our families, we must know the truth. In order to restore our communities, we must know the truth. In order to heal ourselves, we must know the truth. In order to help ourselves, we must know the truth. In order to free ourselves, we must know the truth. Jesus said, "You will know the truth, and the truth will make you free" (John 8:32, RSV).

Oh, if only we knew the truth, our children would stop killing each other. If only we knew the truth, the drug pusher would go bankrupt. If only we knew the truth, our families would survive. If only we knew the truth, our communities would prosper. If only we knew the truth, our churches would thrive.

This is why I am determined to speak the truth about who we are and where we come from. There are some white people who do not want to hear it. There are some black people who do not want to hear it. But I shall speak it anyway, because it is the truth.

And so I pray, "Lord, open my eyes so that I may see your truth. Lord, open my ears so that I may hear your truth. Lord, open my mouth so that I may speak your truth."

The truth is stronger than racism.
The truth is stronger than hate.
The truth is stronger than a lie.
The truth is stronger than evil.
The truth is stronger than despair.
The truth is stronger than lynch mobs.
The truth is stronger than prison bars.
The truth is stronger than guns and bullets.
The truth is stronger than dogs and water hoses.
And the truth is that we are black *and* we are beautiful. Amen.

# Don't Forget Your Heritage
## Deuteronomy 6:4-15

I AM SPEAKING SPECIFICALLY to those of us who are of black African descent today, not to unfavorably exclude anyone, but to favorably include those who have been overlooked. Furthermore, I feel compelled to direct this message particularly to the black church because there is a well-attested crisis of identity among us that I feel the Word of God addresses. You see, I am convinced that the Word of God has a distinctive message to us, as black people, in a way that will save us, heal us, liberate us, and empower us if we listen and respond. Too many times in the church the Word of God is preached as if black people did not exist in the biblical world and as if the problems that especially confront us do not matter. There is a word for us! And if we accept it and believe it, it will transform our situation as a people.

God had a word for the people called Israel. In that word we will also find a message for ourselves. It was a word that came to Israel in the wilderness of Sinai, forty years before they entered the land of promise and about three months after they left the land of Egypt. That word was essentially "do not forget your heritage" (see Deuteronomy 6:12-14). Their heritage was the faith that had been passed down from Abraham, Isaac, and Jacob. Their heritage was the worship of the one, true, and living God. Their heritage was the covenants of promise handed down to them through the teachings of the elders. Their heritage was the memory of deliverance from bondage in Egypt. Their heritage was the law of God received through the hands of God's prophet, Moses; and if they forgot and forsook this heritage, they would suffer disastrous consequences.

The story of Israel demonstrates clearer than any history I know other than our own modern predicament that disaster happens when a people gives up its heritage.

We are an *African* American people. That means that we too have a heritage, not just an American heritage but also an African heritage. It is a special, a peculiar, a precious, and a valuable heritage. It is a heritage that deserves to be lifted up, not pushed back, as black people tend to do when they are made to feel ashamed of their heritage. It is a heritage that deserves to be celebrated, not repressed, as white people tend to do to the black heritage whenever it asserts itself. It is our heritage. Almighty God gave it to us.

Our heritage goes back to the Ibo, the Yoruba, the Hausa, and the Ibibio nations of Nigeria. Our heritage goes back to the Ewe nation of Ghana and Dahomey. Our heritage goes back to the Bacongo of Angola, the Wolof of Senegal and Gambia, the Bambara of Senegal, and the Serere of Gambia. Our heritage goes back to the Mandinka of Gambia and Senegal, the Ashanti of Ghana and the Ivory Coast, and the Fulani of Nigeria, Senegal, and Cameroon. Our heritage goes back to the Fon of Dahomey and the Akan of Ghana. We are an *African* American people. As Israel was warned to retain its heritage, we are also warned to retain ours.

In the Word of God, in Deuteronomy, God says, "Hear, O Israel: the LORD our God is one LORD; and you shall love the LORD your God with all your heart, and with all your soul, and with all your might" (6:4, RSV). In these words, God identifies Godself and decrees how the people of Israel shall respond to the Divine Presence. The reason for this is clear: God did not want the people to forget who God was and how they should live under God. If they forgot, the results would be catastrophic.

We should rejoice in our African heritage, for our African heritage is a God-centered heritage. It is not a world-centered heritage like some religious and philosophical heritages are. It is not a human-centered heritage like some religious and philosophical heritages are. Our heritage is a God-centered heritage. Professor

John S. Mbiti has helped us to see that God is a "High God" in African tradition, the highest of all beings. The Zulu call God "the Great-great-one, Chief of Chiefs and King of Kings." The Bacongo of Angola call God "the Marvel of Marvels." The Yoruba of Nigeria call God "the mighty immovable rock that never dies." The Ashanti of Ghana call God the Eternal One.[1] This same God was revealed to Israel in the wilderness.

As African American people we must beware. There is something very serious and very dangerous happening to us today. In our desire to assimilate and be assimilated into "mainstream American culture" we have jettisoned our traditional African spirituality. Many of us in the midst of our so-called material success believe that we have arrived and that we no longer need God. Now that some of us have good jobs, now that we have two or three cars in our driveways or garages, now that we have two or three bathrooms in the house, some of us have actually concluded that God is dispensable in our lives. One day a black brother actually told me that he did not need to pray and that black people spend too much time praying. Well, if there is anyone here who thinks like that brother, I suggest that you take the blindfold from your eyes. Things are getting bad all over now, and it looks like things are going to get even worse. There is only one way that we are going to survive as a people and that is to let God back into our lives. The only way that we are going to save our families is to let God back into our families. The only way we are going to save our schools is to let God back into our schools. The only way we are going to save our churches is to let God back into our churches. We need to adopt a lifestyle that displays evidence of spiritual discipline and a higher commitment to works that heal and upbuild the human community. This is what I mean by "letting God back in." It is time to recover our God-centeredness. It is time to recover our "Africanness," i.e., a positive attitude about our lost African culture and spiritual heritage.

Contrary to the myths that we have been taught, authentic

---

1. John S. Mbiti, *African Religions and Philosophy* (Garden City, N.Y.: Anchor Books, Doubleday and Co., 1970), pp. 44–46.

African spirituality and religion have not ever been a hodgepodge of superstition, witchcraft, and fetish worship, but rather these have been a highly evolved faith and religion focused on the worship of the true and living God, the same God who was revealed to Akhenaton (1375–1358 B.C.E.), the African king (Egyptian pharaoh) who originated the doctrine of the One God; the same God who was revealed to Moses (1350–1230 B.C.E.), the African prince who led the children of Israel out of bondage. Like the religious heritage of Israel, our heritage is grounded in and centered upon God.

God had something else to say to Israel. God said:

> These words which I command you this day shall be upon your heart; and you shall teach them diligently to your children, and you shall talk of them when you sit in your house, and when you walk by the way, and when you lie down, and when you rise. And you shall bind them as a sign upon your hand, and they shall be as frontlets between your eyes. And you shall write them on the doorposts of your house and on your gates. (Deuteronomy 6:6-9, RSV)

In other words, God commanded the elders of Israel to pass on their heritage of faith and religious instruction to their children. From one generation to the next they were to preserve their tradition and remember God's Word.

I can recall when my parents made me go to Sunday school rehearsal for Christmas, Easter, Mother's Day, and Father's Day programs, and the like. I would have to memorize my lines or Scripture verse so that I would be able to perform on the Sunday of the program. It did not seem like much at the time, but then I grew older. I left home to make it on my own. I gave up the protective shelter of my father and mother's house to mark out my own path in life. I encountered some turbulent and traumatic times, but I am thankful that in the midst of those trying times I remembered some of those Scriptures that I learned. I remembered that

> The Lord is my shepherd, I shall not want; he makes me lie down in green pastures. He leads me beside still waters; he

restores my soul. . . . Even though I walk through the valley of the shadow of death, I fear no evil; for thou art with me; thy rod and thy staff, they comfort me." (Psalm 23:1-4, RSV)

Believe it or not, this process of rehearsal and memorization was very African and biblical. African culture has never been a culture enslaved by the written word. African culture was and is an *oral* culture, a culture of memory and the spoken word. Don't get me wrong. It was African culture that produced the Egyptian hieroglyphics (c. 4600 B.C.E.). It was African (Afroasiatic) culture that produced the Mesopotamian cuneiform (c. 3400 B.C.E.). It was African culture that invented writing. But African culture was and is also a culture of the spoken word handed down from generation to generation, parent to child, child to grandchild. We need to come back to the tradition of passing down our insight and faith to our children. We need to come back to the tradition of passing down our family's history to our children. We need to come back to the tradition of passing on the wisdom of the elders to our children. It is simply not enough to hand our children a book or sit them down in front of a television set. We must come back to sitting our children on our knees or gathering them around us and talking to them about God, talking to them about Jesus, talking to them about what a man is, talking to them about what a woman is, and talking to them about what it means to be African and African American. There is no substitute for that kind of communication. Like the elders of Israel, and the elders of Africa before them, we must pass on our heritage through word and writ.

We finally hear God saying to Israel:

And when the Lord your God brings you into the land which he swore to your fathers, to Abraham, to Isaac, and to Jacob, to give you, with great and goodly cities, which you did not build, and houses full of all good things, which you did not fill, and cisterns hewn out, which you did not hew, and vineyards and olive trees, which you did not plant, and when you eat and are full, then take heed lest you forget the LORD, who brought you out of the land of Egypt, out of the house of bondage." (Deuteronomy 6:10-12, RSV)

The Lord is saying, "Do not forget your history. Do not forget the journey on which I led you. Do not forget where you were as compared to where you will be, and do not forget the Lord who brought you out."

We were enslaved in the antebellum American South for 246 years. We have been free since then for fewer than 140 years. For more than 375 years we have been the targets of racism, prejudice, bigotry, and color discrimination in various shapes and forms. We have not yet reached the "promised land." Despite the belief among some of us that we have arrived, we have not yet reached the promised land. But one day we shall reach the promised land — the land of freedom, the land of equal opportunity, the land of equal rights, and the land of equal justice. When we do, the admonishment given to Israel will hold true for us, "Do not forget the Lord who brought you out."

This is an important warning for us. It is so easy to forget, especially after what has happened to us in this country. You see, something went very wrong for us after the civil rights struggle of the 1950s and 1960s. We believed that we were fighting for integration. And after we achieved passage of the Voting Rights Act, and after we achieved access to public facilities and public schools, and after we won the use of public transportation, we actually thought that we had achieved the lofty goal of integration. But we were tricked. The powers-that-were (and still are) told us that we had achieved integration, but what they actually gave us was assimilation. There is a difference between integration and assimilation. In true integration we gain something when we become part of the whole, but in assimilation we lose something when we become part of the whole. And we have lost so much. We have lost our culture. We have lost our identity. We have lost our history. Our children sit beside white children in some public schools and they all learn about great white people of Europe and America, but they are taught little about great black people of Africa and America. Even when white parents have packed up their children and fled to the suburbs leaving only black and brown children in the inner-city schools, our children are still taught nothing about their own history and heritage. This is assimilation.

Nowadays, however, a new tactic has emerged, and that is to promote assimilation while pretending to promote "pluralism" and "multiculturalism." Don't misunderstand me. Pluralism and multiculturalism are wonderful pursuits — if only we were sincere in our efforts, if only we were aiming for *genuine* pluralism and multiculturalism. But usually when people speak of pluralism or multiculturalism what they really mean is "Yes, let's all get together, but on white terms." This especially happens in church worship settings: "We can write the prayer in Spanish, let's do the responsive reading in Cherokee or Korean, and let's throw in a 'Negro' spiritual and have someone perform a Japanese dance." But when it is all said and done, all we have is a white worship service with ethnic trappings.

In school or classroom settings, the teacher may mention Frederick Douglass, Booker T. Washington (1856–1915), W. E. B. Du Bois, or Martin Luther King, Jr., but there is often no indepth study of these persons and their background, and usually no mention of them is made until Black History month in February. This is a trivialization of our history and culture. This is assimilation. And so many of us are so easily fooled by this type of thing. This is why there are so many of us who have forgotten who we are. We have forgotten our heritage, we have forgotten our identity, we have forgotten our history. Too many of us are black on the outside but white on the inside. Once we forget who we are, it is even easier to forget the Lord who made us. How can some of us ever expect to reach the Promised Land when we have forgotten the Lord already?

The purpose of this message is just to call us back, back to our roots, back to our heritage, back to our history, and back to our identity. I know that this is a hard message. It reminds us of our oppression and challenges us to overcome it when some of us would rather be comfortable in our denial. But it is a true message, and our survival as a people will depend on whether or not we heed it. When Israel held on to its heritage and its cultural identity, it prospered and progressed, but when it abdicated its heritage and cultural identity, it stumbled and fell. So it is with us, the children of Africa. If we want to survive, thrive, and stay alive, we must hold on to that which God has already given to us.

Therefore, I am not ashamed! I am not ashamed of the heritage and identity that is mine. God gave them to me. Therefore, they are good. I am not ashamed! I am not ashamed of the way that I worship the Lord nor of the way that I preach nor of the way that I sing my song. The Spirit of the Lord is moving me, and I yield to the Spirit. I am not ashamed!

Furthermore, I am not ashamed of who I am nor what I look like. I am not ashamed of my deep chocolate color. It is a beautiful color, and I am thankful that I do not have to spend money on tanning lotions and lie around in the sun to have it. God has already given me a beautiful hue. I am not ashamed of my short curly hair. It does not require sprays and creams to hold it in place. When I comb my hair in the morning, it stays in place all day long. I am not ashamed of my broad, flat nose and wide nostrils. They enable me to take in all of God's good air (if only I could find some out here in Los Angeles). I am not ashamed of my thick, full lips; after all, they give me a place to put my moustache. Seriously though, all I am saying is that I am not ashamed of the way God made me, and neither should you be! I am not ashamed of what God has given me, and neither should you be.[2]

For these reasons we celebrate our identity even though there are those who would like for us to forget who we are. We celebrate our history, even though there are those who would like for us to forget our journey. We celebrate our heritage even though there are those who would like for us to forget what God has given us. For when we remember, we stay rooted. When we remember, we stay grounded. When we remember, we stay strong. When we remember, we stay connected. When we remember, we stay balanced. When we remember, we stay whole. The storms may rage against us, the winds may batter us, the flood waters may assault us, but we will survive, we will thrive, we will stay alive because we choose to remember and refuse to forget.

---

2. Inspired by a sermon preached by the Rev. Cornelius Henderson.

# Uncovering the Truth

### Psalm 68:31

I RECALL that when I was a child growing up in an "integrated" school system I learned that "in fourteen hundred ninety-two Columbus sailed the ocean blue" and shortly thereafter "discovered" America, or so they said. Actually, it was a "theft" rather than a discovery. How can someone "discover" something that is already known by others and that belongs to them? If what Columbus did was a discovery, then I think I'll go to our parking lot and "discover" one of those Mercedes Benzes or BMWs. Nevertheless, the questionable Columbus discovery myth is what I was taught in school. Even though Christopher Columbus (1451–1506) was the harbinger of Native American genocide and African enslavement, my teachers portrayed him as a hero. Even now, some groups out of rank insensitivity with respect to the damage that Columbus and his followers did are planning nevertheless to celebrate the five-hundredth anniversary of his arrival in the so-called New World. The Columbus myth is just one of the ways that a racist society perpetuates the lie of white European superiority. The truth of the matter is this — and this is something that my teachers never told me — that about 2293 years before "fourteen hundred and ninety-two" when "Columbus sailed the ocean blue" there were black people from North Africa who sailed around the southern tip of Africa and crossed the Atlantic Ocean in ships of their own construction and landed at sites along the American Gulf Plain and in Central America and Mexico.

This was the first encounter between Nubian-Egyptian seafarers and the great Olmec civilization (1200 B.C.E.–325 B.C.E.) of Mexico.

It was during this time (800–700 B.C.E.) that the Twenty-fifth Egyptian Dynasty, also known as the Ethiopian Dynasty, was flourishing in Upper and Lower Egypt and Cush (biblical Ethiopia or present-day Sudan).[1] The evidence of mummification, stepped pyramids, massive stone heads with Negroid features, hieroglyphic writings, statuettes, skeletal remains with trepannated skulls, and other manifestations of ninth–seventh century B.C.E. Nubian-Egyptian technology within the Olmec culture attest to the African presence in the ancient Americas.[2] The Nubian-Egyptian pharaohs Piankhi (751–716 B.C.E.), Shabaka (c. 712 B.C.E.), and Tirhakah (710–644 B.C.E., see 2 Kings 19:9) presided over a cultural renaissance in Egypt and Cush that even reached across the Atlantic Ocean.[3]

About 182 years before Columbus's voyage (1310–1311 C.E.), black people from West Africa also made a journey from the motherland to the New World. According to Ivan Van Sertima, this was the Mandingo King Abubakari II of Mali and his entourage.[4] Therefore, the first time black people came to the Americas they came not as slaves but as adventurers, explorers, and builders. These African mariners of ancient and medieval times were the first to encounter the native populations of the Americas; and the encounter was mutually beneficial, for it resulted not in conquest but in an exchange of culture. The impact of this encounter became diffused throughout Mesoamerica and Mexico. Even now the pyramids of the Incas in Peru (1200–1527 C.E.), and the pyramids of the Aztecs (1325–1520 C.E.) and the Mayans

---

1. See Ivan Van Sertima, *They Came before Columbus* (New York: Random House, 1976), pp. 30–33, 123–138, 155, 173–174. See also J. A. Rogers, *Sex and Race: Negro-Caucasian Mixing in All Ages and All Lands,* vol. 1, *The Old World* (St. Petersburg: Helga M. Rogers, 1952; reprint 1968), pp. 268–272; Cheikh Anta Diop, *The African Origins of Civilization: Myth or Reality?* trans. Mercer Cook (Westport, Conn.: Lawrence Hill and Co., 1974), p. 116.

2. Ivan Van Sertima, *They Came before Columbus,* pp. 155–157.

3. Ibid., pp. 123–141.

4. Ibid., pp. 26, 37–49, 85.

(2500 B.C.E.–1697 C.E.) in southern Mexico stand as a testimony to ancient African influences.[5]

One day I heard a well-known author trying to explain why the pyramids of North Africa were so similar in design and technology to the pyramids in Peru and Mexico even though they are more than ten thousand miles apart and built about five thousand years ago.[6] Of course, it did not occur to him that an ancient black African people could be so culturally sophisticated and technologically advanced that they could build seacraft able to get them from Africa to the Americas more than two millennia before Columbus. His theory was that aliens from outer space visited both North Africa and the Americas and showed the "primitive" peoples in these places how to build the pyramids. The truth of the pyramids is amazing, yes, but not that amazing. The same African black people who were technologically advanced enough to build the pyramids of Egypt and the Sudan were also advanced enough to build ships that could take them across the Atlantic where they intermingled with Native American nations and shared with them aspects of African culture.

On this occasion in which we are celebrating our history and heritage as African Americans, I would like to deal with truths like these, truths about our past that have been hidden from us down through the years. I am taking on a most difficult task at this time. Not only have these truths been hidden from us through the years, but many of us have been conditioned to reject these truths once they have been brought to the surface. I am presenting you with a challenge to think more deeply than usual upon my message and to consider seriously what I will say to you today. If you rise to this challenge, then I guarantee that what I say to you today will change your perspective on yourself and on our experience as black people in America.

There appears to be a conspiracy in operation, one that has been

---

5. Ibid., pp. 155–157.
6. His remarks were based upon the kind of theories found in Erich von Daniken, *Chariots of the Gods? Unsolved Mysteries of the Past*, trans. Michael Heron (New York: Putnam, 1970), and Lee Gladden and Vivianne Cervantes Gladden, *Heirs of the Gods: A Space Age Interpretation of the Bible* (New York: Rawson-Wade Publishing Co., 1978), pp. 180–183.

in operation for years and years, to hide or deny the significant and indispensable role that black people of African descent have played in history. As an outgrowth of this conspiracy, black people are either rendered invisible or negligible in all education and communication. The history textbook writers are not the only ones guilty of this. The encyclopedia bookmakers, the Bible commentary writers, the Sunday school literature publishers, many public and private school teachers, and even the Hollywood moviemakers are all participants in this effort to deny or hide the black African presence in history.

Some time ago, an old movie was shown on television. The name of that movie was *Spartacus,* starring Kirk Douglas. Spartacus was a "Greek" gladiator who led a violent uprising (73–71 B.C.E. in Italy) against the ancient Roman empire. As far as I can tell, Kirk Douglas, the actor playing the starring role in the movie, is a North American white man. But Spartacus, the actual historical person who lived and died in the Roman empire, was by ancestry a North African black man.[7]

There was another movie called *Cleopatra.* In this movie the role of Cleopatra was played by Elizabeth Taylor. Again a problem. Elizabeth Taylor, as far as I can tell, is a European-American white woman, but Cleopatra, the actual historical person who ruled Egypt and changed the Roman empire, was a North African black woman.

I have seen two movies about Moses. First was Cecil B. De-Mille's *The Ten Commandments,* starring Charlton Heston, and later *Moses, the Lawgiver,* starring Burt Lancaster. Again, both Charlton Heston and Burt Lancaster are North American white

---

7. Robert H. deCoy, *The Blue Book Manual of Nigritian History: American Descendants of African Origins* (Los Angeles: Nigritian, 1969), p. ix. Appian (95–165 C.E.), the Alexandrian Egyptian historian, said that Spartacus was "a Thracian by birth" (*The Civil Wars* 1.116; see *Appian's Roman History,* vol. 3, trans. Horace White [New York: G. P. Putnam's Sons, 1933], p. 215). Thrace (modern-day northeastern Greece and southern Bulgaria) was an Egyptian colony (perhaps like Colchis). The black population was established there in the 1930s or 1920s B.C.E. after that region's conquest by the pharaoh Senwosre I (d. 1935 B.C.E.), also known as Sesōstris I. For a discussion of Sesōstris and Thrace see Martin Bernal, *Black Athena: The Afroasiatic Roots of Classical Civilization,* vol. 2: *The Archaeological and Documentary Evidence* (New Brunswick, N.J.: Rutgers University Press, 1991), pp. 25, 226–228, 234–235, 244–245, 271.

men, but Moses, the actual historical person who led the children of Israel out of Egypt, was an Egyptian-Hebrew black man.

I am convinced that it is necessary to expand our thinking on our own history and heritage in order to be transformed today. We, as a people, cannot find healing, wholeness, and salvation until we have discarded the damaging falsehoods that we have been programmed to believe about ourselves. I pray that this brief investigation of our Scripture text can help us achieve the transformation that we need.

In Psalm 68, where we find our Scripture text, we have various exhortations just to praise the Lord. We are told to praise the Lord because God is "Father of the fatherless and protector of widows" (v. 5, RSV). Praise the Lord because God "gives the desolate a home to dwell in" and God "leads out the prisoners to prosperity (v. 6, RSV). Praise the Lord because God is the one "who daily bears us up" (v. 19, RSV) and the one who "will shatter the heads of his enemies" (v. 21, RSV). What we see here in the Psalm 68 is a tradition of praising the Lord.

One of the things that makes worship in the African and African American traditions so unique is that we give a large place to just praising the Lord. Oh, yes, it is true that there are some churches in the black community who feel that they are too "sophisticated" to praise the Lord. They feel that worship should be "dignified" and quiet, the way the white folks across town worship. These are churches that are rapidly dying out because their worship seems so lifeless and boring. But in those African American churches that have held on to their heritage, that have held on to their tradition, praising the Lord fills the sanctuary. They will even tell you themselves, "ain't no harm to praise the Lord." Some people want to call it "emotionalism," some people want to call it "escapism," some people want to call it "classlessness," but it is none of these things. It is simply being ourselves and letting in the Holy Spirit. Besides, God has brought us too far not to praise God. God has done too much for us not to praise God. God has been too good to us not to praise God. If we have breath in our bodies, if the blood is flowing warmly through our veins, if we are able to move about and have our being, if we are clothed in our right minds, we ought to just praise the Lord!

It was in the midst of all of this praise that the psalmist eventually says, "Let bronze be brought from Egypt; let Ethiopia hasten to stretch out her hands to God" ([v. 31, RSV] Hebrew: *Shema-nim*, "bronze," also translates as "princes," e.g., KJV). In other words, not only are the people exhorted to praise the Lord, but they, especially Egypt and Ethiopia, are further urged to render unto God a praise offering.

Believe it or not, giving is part of our praise. Praise is not just something we do with our lips; praise is also something that we do with our substance and ourselves. We praise God when we give of our financial resources. This is why the psalmist says, "Let bronze be brought from Egypt." We praise God when we give of our bodies, minds, and souls. This is why the psalmist says, "Let Ethiopia hasten to stretch out her hands to God." Praise is the rendering of our all and all to God. Our whole lives together with all that we have should be just one big praise offering to God. God is therefore using the psalmist to call the people of Egypt and Ethiopia to total commitment just as God is still calling us today.

But the key point I want to make this morning — and this may be the point that shocks you — is that the psalmist's call to the Egyptians and the Ethiopians is especially significant for us because both the Egyptians and the Ethiopians were North African black people. Both Egypt and Ethiopia in biblical times were thoroughly black countries. Many people do not seem to realize this. The Hollywood moviemakers certainly do not seem to realize this. The people who draw the pictures in our Sunday school literature do not seem to realize this either. A lot of Bible scholars and Bible commentary writers also do not seem to realize this. But it is true. Anytime the Bible talks about the Egyptians and the Ethiopians, it is talking about black African people, people who looked just like you and me. And I'll tell you something else. The ancient Hebrews were also black people. When Moses led the Hebrew people out of bondage in Egypt after four hundred and thirty years, he was leading a black people out from among a black people. The world of the Bible was a black African world.

Do not misunderstand what I am saying. The message of Psalm 68 is, indeed, for all people, whether they are black, brown, red, yellow, or white. All people ought to submit to the Lord, all people ought to praise the Lord, and all people ought to render their whole selves and their whole substance to the Lord. It matters not who we are or where we come from; the Lord is God and God is worthy of all praise!

One of the things that I am trying to show is that there are black people in the Bible. There are, in fact, more black people in the Bible than any other people.

If we were to go back to the tenth chapter of Genesis, verses 6-20, we have the names of thirty biblical nations. All of these nations were black countries. We know this because they are all descended from Ham, the father of all black African peoples. Even the name "Ham" means "black" (Egyptian: *Khem*; Hebrew: *Chem*, "burnt," "hot," "heated").

We can go back even further to Adam and Eve, the first man and the first woman, who were black people. Even the scientists, the archaeologists, and the paleontologists are admitting that the first human beings were African blacks. Even though many of them do not accept the biblical account of the Creation, they still cannot escape the truth that Africa was the cradle of both humanity and civilization.

There is the story that everyone from Adam to Ham was white, but in the ninth chapter of Genesis, as the story goes, Noah allegedly cursed Ham and turned him black. Thus was the beginning of an accursed black race. This story is a racist lie. First of all, Noah's curse did not turn Ham black. Ham was already black. As a matter of fact, Noah was black. Ham's mother was black. And Ham's brothers, Shem and Japheth, were also black. Everyone all the way back to Adam and Eve was black. Instead of being a curse, being black is a blessing. It was God's will from the very beginning. Second, Noah's curse was not really upon Ham but upon Canaan, Ham's son. Although the Genesis text does not make this clear, Noah's curse upon Canaan was for Canaan's disobedience (Genesis 9:25-27). It explains why Canaan was conquered by Israel when Israel entered the promised land (Joshua 3:10). Still, some people have tried to make this Scripture explain why black people from Africa were made slaves in America. This Scripture has absolutely nothing to do with that. Black people in Africa became slaves in America because they were betrayed by the white-skinned strangers who one day appeared on African shores. Remember, the title of this message is "Uncovering the Truth."

Yes, the message of the psalmist is for all people regardless of race or color, but it is still significant that the primary audience of the message was black people. For too long our white brothers and sisters have acted as if God spoke only to them and that they could impart a secondhand word to us any way and any time they chose. Unfortunately, too many white people saw themselves as the primary recipients and stewards of God's holy revelation. I want us to know that God also spoke directly to black people in the Bible (see also Psalm 87:4; Isaiah 11:11; Isaiah 18:1-2; Isaiah 19:21-22). I want us to know that most of the people God spoke to in the Old Testament would today be considered black people. We no longer have to settle for crumbs from the white folks' table. No, God has prepared a banquet table for us. God has invited us to sit down and feast upon God's Word. The exhortation to the Egyptians and the Ethiopians is our evidence.

Just as God called Egypt and Ethiopia to a life of praise through self-surrender, God is still calling us, the distant children of Egypt and Ethiopia, to this same commitment. But there is something getting in the way today. We are not as spiritual as we used to be. We are not as God-centered as we used to be. We are not as faithful as we used to be. It is because we have neglected or forgotten our heritage. It is because we have forsaken our roots. It is because we have been deceived and miseducated. And still too many black people are trying to be something that they are not. By becoming our true selves again, we can recover our true identities. Is it not time to be authentic? Therefore, we must begin reading the Bible with new eyes. We must begin recovering our own history. We must begin resurrecting our own heritage. We cannot know whose we are without knowing who we are.

This is why we have embarked upon this journey through history. We want to recapture that vital role that we have played in history. Regrettably, we have been lied to and deceived so much. When we have truly discovered our history, when we really come to know who we are, then we can truly praise the Lord. We can praise the Lord for what God has given us. We can praise the Lord for how God has made us. We can praise the Lord for the journey over which God has brought us. We can praise the Lord for where we are going.

So then let us no longer be deceived by the images of Hollywood. Let us no longer be deceived by the pictures in our Sunday school books. Let us no longer be deceived by the portraits hanging on the walls of some of our churches. Let us no longer be deceived by the drawings on the stained-glass windows of some of our churches. There are black people like us between the pages of our Bibles and the pages of ancient history itself. God spoke to them just as God is still speaking to us today.

This is the truth that we want to uncover.

God has always had a word for us.

In the fertile basins of Egypt, God had a word for us.

Beneath the cataracts of the Nile, God had a word for us.

In the black lands of the Sudan, God had a word for us.

Along the lush banks of the Kamby Bolongo, God had a word for us.[8]

In the volcanic shadow of Kilimanjaro, God had a word for us.

In the breezy hills of Haiti, God had a word for us.

In the warm waters of the Bahamas, God had a word for us.

In the blood-stained cotton fields of Alabama, God had a word for us.

In the torrid tobacco patches of Kentucky, God had a word for us.

In the tear-watered sugar cane fields of Louisiana, God had a word for us.

And God still has a word for us, the descendants of Egypt and Ethiopia: "Let bronze be brought out of Egypt, let Ethiopia hasten to stretch out her hands to God" (Psalm 68:31, RSV).

---

8. "Kamby Bolongo," the Gambia River in Alex Haley's *Roots* (Garden City, N.Y.: Doubleday and Co., 1976), p. 4.

# What We Once Were, We Can Be Again

### Genesis 10:6-20 and Genesis 11:1-9

M OST OF US KNOW about the Great Sphinx and the pyramid of Cheops, which were built around 2500 B.C.E. in the area now known as Gizeh, near Cairo. We have at least seen drawings and pictures of the Great Sphinx and the pyramid of Cheops in various places. We may also be familiar with the other pyramids of Egypt like the pyramids of Khaf-Re and Men-Kau-Re. Those of us who are interested in history and archaeology may also be familiar with the great ancient city of Thebes (Nahum 3:8-9), the capital city of ancient Egypt around 2040 B.C.E. (now the site of modern-day Luxor), and we may also be familiar with the ancient temple of Karnak in the east part of Thebes, where scholars go to study the magnificent hieroglyphic writings on the walls and columns of the temple. People know that these and other buildings found in North Africa are marvels of architecture and technology showing an advanced stage of development in the areas of science, physics, mathematics, and art. When scholars and other people come from a great many miles around to look at the great pyramids and temples of Egypt and the Sudan, they realize without a doubt that these structures were the work of a highly sophisticated, technologically advanced, culturally superior people. But what many people do not realize or admit is that these marvels of engineering, these technological masterpieces, were, from design to construction, the work of black people.

I have been saying it for the past several years — that one of the great cover-ups of the modern American white-dominated and white-controlled educational systems is to ignore the fact that the ancient Egyptians, the ancient Ethiopians, the ancient Mesopotamians, the ancient Hebrews, and the ancient Arabians were all black people of African descent, and that these ancient black people were the architects and builders of world civilization and culture.

This is not to deny that Europeans and white Asians[1] have also made significant and original contributions to the development of world culture and civilization, but it is to overthrow the deeply ingrained notion that black people of African descent have made little or no contribution at all.

Yes, the truth of the matter is — and we can prove this — is that white people were not the original inventors of science and mathematics; black people were.

White people were not the original inventors of art and music; black people were.

White people were not the original inventors of letters and writing; black people were.

White people were not the original inventors of medicine and health sciences; black people were.

White people were not the original inventors of metallurgy and masonry; black people were.

White people were not the original inventors of chemistry and pharmacology; black people were.

---

1. The term "white Asians" is used by Chancellor Williams, who also uses the synonymous terms "Asiatic Caucasians" and "Euro-Asians." He means both Caucasian immigrants from ancient Europe who settled in the ancient Near East and their descendants. Therefore, his use of the term "Asian" is primarily a *geographical* referent. Nevertheless, there is potential for confusion because some scholars use the term "Asian" as primarily an *ethnic* referent for some indigenous inhabitants of the ancient Near East, and even Chancellor Williams allows for this usage. "Asian" in this latter sense could also mean people with an African bloodline. Consequently, "Eurasian" or "Euro-Asian" could refer to people with mixed Caucasian and African ancestry. Joel A. Rogers, for example, uses the word "Asian" in this sense and even goes so far as to say that certain ancient Asian (i.e., Eurasian) peoples were "mulattoes." However, it is not altogether clear whether Williams would really disagree with Rogers's classification of some Asian peoples (i.e., Assyrians, Medes, Persians) as "mulattoes" instead of "whites."

See Chancellor Williams, *The Destruction of Black Civilization: Great Issues of a Race from 4500 B.C. to 2000 A.D.* (Chicago: Third World Press, 1987), pp. 39, 65, 77–78, 102–103, 180.

See also J. A. Rogers, *Sex and Race: Negro-Caucasian Mixing in All Ages and All Lands*, vol. 1: *The Old World* (St. Petersburg: Helga M. Rogers, 1952; reprint 1968), pp. 56–57.

White people were not the original inventors of astronomy and navigation; black people were.

White people were not the original developers of philosophy and religion; black people were.

And no matter how hard people try to suppress this truth, the truth is going to come out. As a matter of fact, the truth is coming out all over, and it is coming out right here and right now. It was black people — black people! — not the Greeks, not the Romans, who laid the foundations of modern culture and civilization. We even have evidence for this in the Bible. The Bible is not the only place where we have evidence of the foundational role of black people in world history and civilization, but for us it is the most significant place; and one of those places in the Bible of great significance for us is the passage of Genesis 10:6-20. Now most of us, if we came across this portion of Scripture in our reading, would probably rush through it without thinking. For one thing it does not seem, on the surface, to tell us much, and what it does tell us doesn't seem all that relevant today. Yet this passage tells us a whole lot about ourselves, and if we would take the time to explore it we would discover some wonderful truths.

Let me illustrate. In the tenth chapter of Genesis, in the eighth verse, we are introduced to a man named Nimrod, the son of Cush, who was the son of Ham. Now Ham had three other sons besides Cush. Their names are listed in Genesis 10:6. They are Mizraim, Put, and Canaan. Each one of these sons became the father of a country that went by the same name. Therefore, the descendants of Ham became the countries of Mizraim, Put, Canaan, and Cush. Today we know these countries by different names. Mizraim is now called Egypt. Put is now called Libya. Canaan is now called Palestine, and Cush is now called Sudan. The modern-day country of Sudan, however, was known in Bible times as Ethiopia, not to be confused with present-day Ethiopia (known in Bible times as Punt).[2] Nimrod is therefore, from a biblical perspective, the son of Ethiopia, and according to the Scripture, Nimrod, the son of

---

2. Cheikh Anta Diop, *The African Origin of Civilization: Myth or Reality?* (Westport, Conn.: Lawrence Hill and Co., 1974), pp. 145–147.

Ethiopia, was "the first man on earth to be called a mighty man." We learn by reading on that Nimrod was a mighty hunter before the Lord. In fact, he was such a mighty hunter that his reputation became proverbial. That is why people said, "Like Nimrod, a mighty hunter before the LORD" (v. 9, RSV). Furthermore, we learn that Nimrod was also the builder of a great kingdom comprised of such famous cities as Babel and Nineveh.

So then Nimrod was a great ruler, provider, and builder. And this is important. But Nimrod, the son of Ethiopia, is important to us not just because he was the first man on earth to be a mighty man (i.e., hunter, builder, ruler, and provider) but also because he was an African black man. Someone will ask, "Pastor, how do you know that Nimrod was an African black man?" I know because the Bible says that Nimrod was the son of Cush and Cush was the son of Ham and Ham was the father of all black African peoples. As a matter of fact, the very name Ham (*Khem*) is an Egyptian-Hebrew word that means "blackened by the sun."[3] Therefore, because Nimrod was the son of Cush, the son of Ham, we know that he was an African black man. This is highly significant. The first man on earth to be a mighty man was a black man. And if the first man on earth to be a mighty man was a black man, then the first people on earth to be a mighty people were black people, and the first nations on earth to be mighty nations were black nations.

You see, black people need not wonder about what God wants and intends for us to be. All we have to do is look at King Nimrod, the son of Cush, a ruler, a builder, and a provider, and we will see what God wanted and intended for us to be. Nimrod was *not* there to build and provide for some other people, but for his own people. Obviously, something has happened to us along the way, but I am convinced that what God wanted and intended for us to be, we can still be. First, however, we must learn who and what we once were, because it is only by learning who and what we once were that we will be able to go forward and become what we ought to

---

3. See Cheikh Anta Diop, *The African Origin of Civilization*, pp. 7, 247. See also Walter Arthur McCray, *The Black Presence in the Bible: Discovering the Black and African Identity of Biblical Persons and Nations* (Chicago: Black Light Fellowship, 1990), pp. 54, 148.

be. Nimrod, the son of Cush, shows us who and what we once were. What more can we say about him? For this we need to go to Genesis 11:1-9. There we discover that Nimrod was the one responsible for engineering the construction of the famous Tower of Babel. According to the Scripture, this was a time when the earth had only one language and few words. People migrated from Africa to a place in Mesopotamia called Shinar, and there they decided to build a tower that would reach all the way up into the heavens. They wanted to build a tower so great that they would make a name for themselves as a great unified nation.

Because I am an African American striving to be more African every day, I want my people to know that they are a great people and that we have nothing to be ashamed of. I want my people to know that we have a great history and legacy and that we have made a tremendous contribution to the history and development of the world. But I also want my people to know that without God we are nothing, and whatever we try to do or accomplish without God will falter, fail, and fall.

These were black people who started out under the leadership of Nimrod to build the great ziggurat pyramid known as the Tower of Babel, but at least one mistake they made when they started out was to build something for their own glory rather than the glory of God. It is a common human failing to place self and selfish aspirations before God and the achieving of God's will. We have made this mistake by forsaking our own heritage and culture in an effort to imitate white people. We have made this mistake by laying aside the African ideals of community and cooperation for the European-American ideals of individualism and competition. Too many black people have made this mistake of identifying with the oppressors rather than with the oppressed. We have made this mistake by pursuing what we want for us rather than what God wants for us.

So then, when God came down, as the Scripture says, to check out what these folks were doing, God saw that if they were allowed to continue that they would get carried away with their success and become proud and arrogant. "This is only the beginning of what they will do," God said, "and nothing that they propose will now be impossible for them" (Genesis 11:6, RSV). It is not that God does not want us to accomplish great things, for God does want us to accomplish great things and God will help us accomplish great things. It is just that God does not want us to get caught in the trap of thinking that we can achieve real success without God's help. This is a trap that has ensnared many of us.

So God and the heavenly host came down and confused their language and scattered them all over the face of the earth (Genesis 11:7-9). The people of Babel were confused and scattered because they became carried away with the quest for fame and power. This continues to happen to us from time to time, but today we are also confused and scattered by other people who are carried away with the quest for fame and power. And I want to be very clear about this. Although we are responsible for pulling ourselves together, we are not entirely to blame for what has happened to us. We have been confused and scattered by colonialism. We have been confused and scattered by racism. We have been confused and scattered by bigotry and discrimination. We have been confused and scattered by miseducation and assimilation. But the message of the Scriptures to us is regardless of the reasons why we are confused and scattered, we can find strength and unity in the Lord.

Therefore, as an African American who is striving to be more African every day, I want us to become the great people that we started out to be — great leaders, great builders, and great providers for our families and our communities. But most of all, I want us to be great in the Lord, because if we are great in the Lord then we shall be great indeed.

As the Bible and history show, there was a time when we walked the face of the earth as kings and queens, princes and princesses. What we once were, we can be again.

There was a time when we were the masters of the arts and the sciences. What we once were, we can be again.

There was a time when we were the spiritual leaders of the world. What we once were, we can be again.

There was a time when we held the light of knowledge and education. What we once were, we can be again.

There was a time when we were the models of community and family life. What we once were, we can be again.

To tell the truth, we are already on our way to being what we once were, because the Spirit of the Lord is at work in the church and in the world redeeming God's broken, oppressed, and victimized people. God is making us what God wants us to be.

This, by the way, is my personal desire. I just want to be what God wants me to be. I want to walk the way God wants me to walk. I want to talk the way God wants me to talk. I want to act the way God wants me to act. I want to work the way God wants me to work. I want to live the way God wants me to live.

My prayer is: "Lord, just give me more of your wisdom, just give me more of your strength, just give me more of your grace, just give me more of your spirit, so that I can be what you want me to be."

Are you willing, my people, to be what God wants you to be? Then let us come home to God. Let us come home to the Scriptures, let us come home to a prayer life, let us come home to worship, let us come home to Christian service, let us come home to an African consciousness, and God will transform us into the people that God wants us to be. Amen.

# A Black Man
# to the Rescue

## Isaiah 37:8-13

W ELCOME TO THIS CELEBRATION of African American history and heritage. Today I want to talk about a black man
in the Bible named Tirhakah, king of Ethiopia. Tirhakah was a
black man whom we find mentioned in two places in the Old Testament; first in 2 Kings 19:9 and here in our text for today, Isaiah
37:9. Tirhakah lived from about 710 to 644 B.C.E. and was known
as a great military leader and empire builder. He became king of
Cush (or biblical Ethiopia, the territory of modern-day Sudan) at
the age of sixteen and was thus known as "the boy king."[1] During his twenty-five-year reign, his kingdom became the largest
in Northern Africa. He was such a powerful military force that
the mention of his name struck terror in the hearts of would-be
conquerors.

Before we proceed further with our discussion about Tirhakah,
king of Ethiopia, I feel that we need to deal with the fact that many
of us in the church of Jesus Christ do not realize the significant role
that black men and black women have played in biblical history.
When I was a child growing up in church and in Sunday school,
I was not even told that there are black people in the Bible. Even

---

1. See Ivan Van Sertima, *They Came before Columbus* (New York: Random House,
1976), pp. 129–138, 146. See also John G. Jackson, *Introduction to African Civilizations*, with an introduction by John Henrik Clarke (Secaucus, N.J.: Citadel Press, 1970),
pp. 115–116.

now, when I go to some churches (and this includes black churches) and tell people that there are black people in the Bible and that black people have played a significant role in biblical history, folks look at me as if I were from another planet. But the truth of the matter is that the Bible represents a world before color prejudice and a world that had a very favorable attitude toward black people.

It may come as a surprise for some of us to learn that when we read of the Egyptians and the Ethiopians in our Bibles, we are in fact reading about North African black people. People are especially surprised to learn that the Egyptians were black, because historians and movie producers have for years portrayed them as white. Furthermore, we have so many white-skinned Egyptians in modern-day Egypt that we can easily get the impression that the way Egyptian people look now is the way that they have always looked. The truth is that way back in ancient and biblical times before white-skinned peoples from the forests, caves, and mountains of Europe arrived and began interbreeding with the darker-skinned peoples of Africa and Asia, the Egyptians, like the Ethiopians, were a black- and brown-skinned African race who looked like most of us in this sanctuary. Even more surprising to many of us is the knowledge that the early Hebrews and Israelites, whom we read about throughout the Bible, were also a people of black African descent. This is hard for some to believe, because when we look at modern-day Jews, Israelis, or Hebrew-speaking peoples, we see mostly white people.

Furthermore, every time we see portraits or drawings of biblical peoples, we see them portrayed as white Europeans. Even now when we look at the pictures in our Sunday school literature or look at the portraits of biblical personalities hanging on the walls of our churches, we do not see anyone who looks like any of us. We need to realize that when we speak of ancient and biblical people that we are speaking of times way before the seventh century B.C.E., when white-skinned European people began to infiltrate, intermingle with, invade, and conquer the dark-skinned peoples of Asia and North Africa. And we need to realize that even in the seventh century B.C.E. the process was just beginning. The Afro-

Asian hemisphere did not become white overnight, and it is still not completely white.

Like most of you, I can recall very closely following the crisis in the Persian Gulf and the Middle East (January 16–February 27, 1991). Just like you I beheld numerous images flash across my TV screen — images of people from the Middle East, Iraq, Israel, Jordan, Iran, Saudi Arabia. As I watched I saw many people who could easily blend in with us, but I waited for just one indigenous blue-eyed blond or brunet white person to show up on my TV screen. One never did show up, yet America has been led to believe that thousands of years ago the whole of the Old and New Testament worlds were populated by white Europeans and that even Jesus himself was a white-skinned, blue-eyed blond with small, European features. I believe that it is time to challenge such misrepresentations of history.

But before we go any further, let us deal with the question of why to raise this challenge in the first place. Why rock the boat? Why take the risk of offending people, especially white people? First of all, who says that white people should never be offended, especially when they are wrong? But there is a more important reason why we must raise the challenge, and it has to do with what is happening to black people today. We are dying today. "Dying of what?" you may ask. We are dying of lack of self-esteem. One of the reasons why so many of us are drugging and drinking ourselves to death, one of the reasons why so many of our children are shooting and stabbing one another to death, one of the reasons why so many of our men are attacking and brutalizing our women, one of the reasons why so many of our women are unfairly castigating and slandering our men, one of the reasons why so many of our children are suffering neglect and abuse, one of the reasons why so many of us have dropped out of society, is widespread lack of self-esteem. And the reason for this lack of self-esteem is that we have believed the lie that we as a people are nothing, and that we have made no meaningful contributions to history and the march of civilization. The truth of the matter is that black people in distant African antiquity were the ones who started civilization. We were the ones who invented culture. We were the ones who fashioned the arts and sciences and watched as they were passed on to the rest of humanity. Therefore, for the sake of our children, for the sake of ourselves, for the sake of our future, and for the sake of the truth, we must talk about the presence and role of black people in all history including biblical history.

With all of this in mind, I want to return now to talk about Tirhakah, the king of Ethiopia. The story begins one day in the year 691 B.C.E., when Hezekiah, the king of Judah, looks up and discovers that the city of Judah is surrounded by his enemies, the Assyrians. Just when things are going well in the city, Hezekiah looks up and sees trouble all around. You see, prior to this invasion, the city of Judah had undergone a religious revival under the leadership of King Hezekiah. They had torn down all of their idols. They had torn down all of their altars dedicated to false gods. They had cleansed the temple, and the whole city had turned back to the worship of the one, true, and living God. Consequently, God was blessing them with such prosperity and unity as had not been seen since the days of David the king. Just when things were going so well, here comes the enemy.

Isn't that just like the enemy, to come when things seem to be going so well? We see that in our own history. One of the falsehoods that has been perpetuated about our heritage is that when white Europeans came to Africa, we were only primitives, savages, or heathens running around naked in the jungle and that the best thing benevolent white people could have done for us was capture us and bring us here to America, "the land of the free and the home of the brave." The truth is that our African forebears were not primitives, savages, or heathens running around naked in the jungle, but were citizens of highly developed and advanced cultures and civilizations. The West African kingdoms of Ghana (not to be confused with the former "Gold Coast," renamed Ghana in 1957 by the government of President Kwame Nkrumah, 1909–1972), Mali, Ashanti, Songhay, Mossi states, Hausa states, and Congo were once flourishing empires whose achievements in the arts and sciences put the European nations to shame. Yes, there were some ignoble moments in precolonial African history. There were internecine wars, conflicts, and territorial disputes between

African nations. There were some cases of demagoguery, greed, and corruption in African governments just as there have been in other governments. There were even a few West African kings who heedlessly sold black convicted criminals and prisoners of war as slaves to white merchant mariners, but, generally speaking, prosperity and peace were the order of the day. Some of these African nations were at their height.

But just when things were going so well, there came the enemy. The next thing we knew, we were being placed in holding cells, packed into slave ships like sardines in a can, and then hauled across the Atlantic Ocean. What did Jesus say to his disciples? He said, "Watch and pray" (Mark 14:38, RSV). If ever there was a lesson that black people need to learn, it is this one. We must watch and pray not only in times of trouble but also when things are going well. We must watch and pray *especially* when things are going well, for as soon as we let our guard down, the enemy will strike. It was the apostle Peter who said, "Be sober, be watchful. Your adversary the devil prowls around like a roaring lion, seeking some one to devour" (1 Peter 5:8, RSV).

Not only did the Assyrians have Hezekiah and his people surrounded, but the Assyrians also began to taunt and ridicule them. Sennacherib, the king of Assyria, sent a messenger to the people of Judah saying in effect, "On what do you base your confidence, Hezekiah? I know that one of your allies is Egypt, but Egypt is broken and anyone depending on Egypt will be disappointed and defeated. And don't tell me that you are depending upon God. I have conquered the cities of Hamath and Arpad and Sepharvaim [in present-day northern Syria]. Each one of them said that they were depending upon their gods, but where are their gods now?" (Isaiah 36:4-19, author's paraphrase).

You see, church, whenever the Evil One, our adversary, has us hemmed in and surrounded, the Evil One will try to destroy our faith with doubts and fears. The Evil One will try to convince us that we do not have a chance to win the battle, and that we might as well give up. All we have to do is drive around our community, and there they stand, on the street corners, in front of the liquor stores, in the alleyways, young black men who have given up because the

Evil One has said to them, "You don't have a chance." Speaking through the mouth of the public school teacher who failed to teach them their proud heritage or much of anything else and instead programmed them for failure, the Evil One said "You don't have a chance." Speaking through the mouth of the employer who is reserving his jobs for whites while pretending he has no openings for blacks, the Evil One said, "You don't have a chance." Speaking through the mouth of the public official who blames blacks for their own predicament while absolving white society of all guilt, the Evil One said, "You don't have a chance."

But we can take a lesson from Hezekiah. After Hezekiah heard from his enemy's representative he went into the house of the Lord, and from there he sent a message to God's representative asking him to pray. It just so happens that God's representative at this time was Isaiah the prophet, and Isaiah sent a message back to the king saying, "Thus saith the Lord. Do not be afraid. Your enemy is going to fall" (Isaiah 37:6-7, author's paraphrase).

In the end, it is not what our adversary says that counts but what God says, and God still speaks through God's prophets. There is a tendency today to be skeptical of the truth that God still speaks through the mouth of God's prophets. But in critical times such as these we cannot afford such skepticism. It is true that we have had one scandal after another involving TV evangelists and local church preachers, but God still speaks through God's prophets. It is true that we live in an increasingly secular society that discounts the reality of God, but God still speaks through God's prophets. It is true that the church is being held up as an object of ridicule today, but God still speaks through God's prophets. And the word for us today is, "Don't be afraid, your enemy is going to fall." We may be surrounded by racism and bigotry; we may be hemmed in by prejudice and discrimination, but God's word for us is, "Don't be afraid, your enemy is going to fall."

This does not mean that we sit back and do nothing. No, God does not suggest such a course in the Bible. God wants us to build unity and community. God want us to be politically involved. God wants us to be socially active. God wants us to seek economic empowerment. God wants us to educate our children. God wants us to establish safe, loving homes. God wants us to build safe, nurturing neighborhoods. But while we are busy doing all of these things, God's message to us is still, "Don't be afraid, your enemy is going to fall."

God had a plan for the salvation of Hezekiah and the people of Judah, and that plan was going to result in the total destruction of Sennacherib's army. Phase one of God's plan was to have the Assyrian army drawn away from Judah by the threat of another army, the army of Libnah (Isaiah 37:8). When Sennacherib's messenger returned to the Assyrian campsite, he found that the Assyrian forces were gone. They had left to fight this other army from Libnah, which seemed to come out of nowhere. Then, before the Assyrians could dispose of Libnah, they received word that another army was amassing to attack them. This time it was the army of the Ethiopians led by their King Tirhakah, whose army had the reputation of being the fiercest fighting machine in the land (Isaiah 37:9). In desperation, the messenger of Sennacherib returned to Judah and tried one more time to intimidate them into surrender, but Hezekiah just took his threats and laid them before the Lord (Isaiah 37:10-14). Then God sent another word to Hezekiah through his prophet Isaiah saying that "the king of Assyria won't even get close to the city. He won't even be able to shoot any arrow, nor raise any shield, nor set up any siege mound against it. The way he came is the way he is going to return, for God is defending the city to save it" (Isaiah 37:33-35, author's paraphrase). According to the Scripture, Tirhakah and his Ethiopian forces pushed the Assyrians back to the Assyrian camp, where the Assyrians were then mysteriously annihilated by an angel of the Lord (Isaiah 37:36). Sennacherib, the Assyrian king managed to escape to Nineveh, but he was subsequently killed by his own sons while he was worshiping his false god (Isaiah 37:37-38).

The thing we do not want to miss, however, is that when Judah had no other defense, God chose a black man named Tirhakah and a black people called the Ethiopians to come between the Assyrians and Judah. Do you hear what I am saying? When things hung in the balance, when calamity threatened the people, when disaster seemed imminent, God called upon some black people from Africa to save the day. When danger was all around, when all hope seemed lost, when it appeared that there was no escape, God called a black man to the rescue. Tirhakah was his name.

Yes, we had a role to play in salvation history, and this is only one example! The chief point is that if God could use black people in such great ways in the past, God can still use us in great ways today. We have been and can still be instruments of God, instruments of salvation, instruments of healing, and instruments of liberation.

I know that this is hard for some of us to believe. Many of us feel like the people of Judah when they were surrounded by the Assyrians. We do not feel like instruments of anything constructive. We feel useless and hopeless. Furthermore, wherever we go in the global village, it appears that the enemy has its foot on our heads. When we go to South Africa, the enemy has its foot on our heads. When we go to Central America, the enemy has its foot on our heads. When we go to the Caribbean, the enemy has its foot on our heads. When we go to Harlem, the enemy has its foot on our heads. Right here in South Central Los Angeles, the enemy has its foot on our heads. But in the midst of this hopelessness and oppression, we have a word from the Lord saying, "Our day is coming." Our day is coming because God is a God of justice, the God who rights the wrong, who defends the weak, who sides with the oppressed. Our day is coming because God said, "I make your enemies your footstool" (Psalm 110:1, RSV). Our day is coming because Jesus said, "Blessed are those who hunger and thirst for righteousness, for they shall be satisfied" (Matthew 5:6, RSV). Our day is coming because the apostle said, "Let us not grow weary in well-doing, for in due season we shall reap, if we do not lose heart" (Galatians 6:9, RSV).

And so we ought to keep laboring for justice until our day comes. We ought to keep marching for freedom until our day comes. We ought to keep fighting for the right until our day comes.

Young people, don't let the world discourage you; just fight on until our day comes.

Mothers, don't let the Evil One break your spirit; just press on until our day comes.

Fathers, don't let obstacles drive you to despair; just run on until our day comes.

For when our day comes, God will set enemies to flight and make everything all right.

# The Man Who Lent a Helping Hand

## Jeremiah 39:15-18

E BED-MELECH WAS ONE OF THOSE BIBLICAL PERSONALITIES we do not hear too much about, yet he had a significant role to play in the unfolding of God's will. He is especially important for us during our black history observance, because Ebed-melech himself was a black man. I am convinced that in this day when there is an urgent need for role models for our children it is vitally important to point out notable and exemplary black men and black women in history, and not just in modern and contemporary history but also in ancient and biblical history. Ebed-melech the Ethiopian was one of those notables who should be pointed out for the sake of our children and ourselves.

It is not unusual for the Bible to relate the story of a black person. Most of the characters or personalities of the Bible were black people. Yet for years and years the society that surrounds us has succeeded in hiding the black African identities of these biblical people as part of its program to instill within us a sense of rootlessness, worthlessness, and "nobodiness." But then there were a few personalities in the Bible whose black African identities were nearly impossible to hide. Ebed-melech the Ethiopian was one of them. Why is his identity as a black man so hard for white scholars to hide? It is simply because the Bible refers to him as "The Ethiopian" or "The Cushite" (as the older translations read). The name "Cushite" is synonymous with the word "Ethiopian," and one thing that even the most racist scholars have not been able to do is hide the fact that the ancient and biblical Ethiopians, like contemporary Ethiopians, were North African black people.[1] And so the story of Ebed-melech the Ethiopian is indisputably the story of a black man.

By the way, everybody has a story, and everyone ought to have an opportunity to celebrate the positive dimensions of his or her story even while admitting the difficulties. One of the chief traits of traditional African society was the practice of storytelling. The children and even the adults would gather around one of the elders or griots who told them the story of their community and of notable individuals. What this did for the community's sense of pride, identity, and corporate self-esteem is beyond calculation. The damage that is done when people are deprived of their story is also beyond calculation.

A short time ago, when I was traveling in South Africa as part of a special mission, we had the opportunity to tour a gold-mining museum and theme park known as Gold Reef City. At the time, I was already distressed and depressed by firsthand observance of the ill effects of South Africa's oppressive apartheid government. Our well-meaning white hosts had taken us to several points of interest in the Johannesburg area, but the juxtaposition of white affluence and black impoverishment left me with a feeling of despair. Things became worse when our tour guide brought us to a point where we paused to hear the story of Gold Reef City and the urban development of South Africa. She told us how a Dutchman named John Harrison came to South Africa in the 1700s and subsequently "discovered" gold. This precipitated a gold rush much like the California gold rush of the 1800s. She then told the story of how towns and villages were established, leading to the development of large industrial centers like Johannesburg.

But as she told the story of South Africa, I kept waiting for her to tell the story of the people who were already there before the gold-hungry invaders came. I kept waiting for her to tell the story of the Xhosa, the Zulu, the Swazi, the Ndebele, the Sotu,

---

1. Indigenous inhabitants of southern Cush (biblical Ethiopia, or the territory of present-day Sudan) were known as "Nubians."

and others of the proud and noble black South African peoples who inhabited the land before it was taken from them by force. *But she did not even mention them, not even once.* It was as if they had never existed. In the relatively brief time that it took for her to tell the story of *white* South Africa, our tour guide managed to exterminate whole races of people. I felt that I had witnessed an ideological genocide. I was so affected that I became physically ill and left the theme park. When a society erases a people's story, that society is only a small step away from eliminating the people themselves. The reason that we are having this black history observance is so that we may tell our story.

There were other black men and women in the Bible besides Ebed-melech. We shall speak of them over the course of the next few weeks. Today we lift up Ebed-melech, who lived in Jerusalem during the time of Jeremiah the prophet (627–580 B.C.E.). He was notable for several reasons.

First, Ebed-melech was available to God. The situation that Ebed-melech found himself in began when Jerusalem came under the threat of destruction from Nebuchadnezzar, king of the Babylonians and the mighty Babylonian war machine (Jeremiah 37:1-10). At that time (598 B.C.E.), Zedekiah was king of Jerusalem and he was looking for a way out. But he wanted out his way, not God's way. Zedekiah's way was to make an alliance with the Egyptians and defeat the Babylonians with their combined military might. But God's way was that Jerusalem forget about the alliance with Egypt, surrender to Babylon, and repent of the sins that got them into trouble in the first place. Zedekiah and his counselors did not want to do this. So God sent a prophet named Jeremiah to warn the people that disaster was coming if they did not do as God had directed and surrender to the Babylonians (Jeremiah 37:11-21; 38:1-3). Naturally, this enraged the king's generals and counselors, so they seized Jeremiah and threw him into a muddy well to starve to death (Jeremiah 38:4-6). God, however, was watching over Jeremiah, and it was certainly not God's will that Jeremiah become a stick-in-the-mud. So God had someone go to the king and report what the king's men had done. God then made the king give permission to that same someone to go

get help and retrieve Jeremiah from the well. That same someone succeeded in pulling Jeremiah from the well and delivered him
to safety. That someone was Ebed-melech the Ethiopian. When
God needed someone to rescue God's servant, Ebed-melech was
available to be used (Jeremiah 38:7-13).

This is really all that God asks of us — not that we be strong and
powerful first, not that we be well-established and well-organized
first, but that we be available to God. If we are available to God
first, then God will give us the strength and power that we need. If
we are available to God first, then God will establish and organize
us for action.

There was no way that a seamstress in Montgomery, Alabama,
named Rosa Parks could have known what she was starting by
refusing to move her tired body to the back of a bus, but God
had chosen her for that moment (December 5, 1955), and she
was available to be used. There was no way she could have antic-
ipated the marshaling of human and material resources that were
necessary for the successful execution of the Montgomery bus boy-
cotts (December 6, 1955–December 21, 1956) and the subsequent
launching of the American civil rights movement, but God had
chosen her to put those wheels into motion, and she was available to be used. Each of us need to ask ourselves this morning, "Is
God summoning me to service? Have I made myself available yet?"
Ebed-melech is our example. He was available.

Ebed-melech is notable also because he was willing to risk his
neck. We have to keep in mind that although Ebed-melech had
the king's permission to rescue Jeremiah, his life would have been
forfeited if his plan had been discovered by the king's generals
and counselors. Ebed-melech trusted in God, and because he did,
he was willing to put his life on the line for what God wanted
(Jeremiah 38:7-13). Ebed-melech the Ethiopian shows us what
countless other servants of God have shown us — that being a
servant of God is risky business. Indeed, we cannot do God's will
without taking risks. There is just no such thing as "playing it safe"
and doing what God wants us to do.

I thought about this while we were in South Africa and a debate
erupted within our racially mixed group about whether or not we

should enter Soweto. Some wanted to go. Some thought that in light of recent events and loss of life in Soweto it was just too dangerous. Those of us who wanted to go thought that it would be a shame to come all that distance from America and not fellowship with our brothers and sisters who lived in Soweto. So there was a split in the group between those who stayed behind and those who went into Soweto. As we entered Soweto, our bus was stopped by South African police. I suppose they wanted to check us out. As I watched policemen armed with automatic rifles walking around our rickety bus, I felt some of the tension on the bus, but I also felt a sense of peace. I felt that it was all right to be taking this kind of risk, for we were doing something for the Lord. As it turned out, we enjoyed a time of fellowship with our brothers and sisters in Soweto (and neighboring Katlehong) and were able to return to Germiston and Benoni before nightfall without our bus breaking down. We can face all sorts of danger with assurance when we are anchored in the will of God.

Ebed-melech is notable also because he was willing to help his "brother." Jeremiah was a Jew, Ebed-melech was an Ethiopian, but still they were brothers in the Lord.[2] Ebed-melech knew that he had to act upon that fact when he saw his brother in trouble. When destruction finally came upon Jerusalem because of their disobedience, God rewarded Ebed-melech by keeping him safe, simply because he trusted in God enough to help his brother (Jeremiah 39:15-18).

If ever we needed a model for our living, it is this one. We must learn to pull together instead of pulling apart. I am convinced that our survival as a people will depend upon it. Unfortunately, we have learned the lessons of self-hate all too well. "Because I hate myself, I hate anyone who looks like me." This is what self-hate is all about. Self-hate is a product of overexposure to racism. The cure for the situation is for us to open ourselves anew to God, who can uniquely assist us in falling in love with ourselves again. After

---

2. As late as the first century C.E., there were people who thought that the Jews and Ethiopians were of the same "race" (Tacitus, *History* 5.2, *The Complete Works of Tacitus*, trans. Alfred John Church and William Jackson Brodribb (New York: Random House, 1942), pp. 657–658.

all, Jesus held up the Old Testament teaching "love your neighbor as yourself" (Matthew 22:39, RSV). We cannot love anyone else until we love ourselves. We cannot help anyone else until we love ourselves. This is why we celebrate blackness. This is why we celebrate Africanness. This is why we are lifting up our own culture and heritage. This is why we are identifying the black presence in the Bible. We must come to love ourselves again, so that we can become a community of love.

While visiting the Transvaal region of South Africa I was speaking to a newfound friend who was a member of the Zulu nation. I am sure that he perceived my interest in aspects of traditional African culture. He favored me by telling me of the Zulu. I was most impressed by what he told me of the Zulu hospitality tradition. "When a stranger enters our community," he told me, "that person automatically becomes a member of the king's family since that person has no relatives within the community. This gives that person all the benefits and protection of the laws of the community. A person must be related to someone in the community to have those protections. So then we have a saying, 'Do that man no harm; he is a child of the king. Do that woman no harm; she is a child of the king.'" What a wonderful tradition that is. It is something that we need to recover as an African people. "Do that brother no harm; he is a child of the king!" "Do that sister no harm; she is a child of the king!" No matter where we are or where we go, God is our king and we are God's children. Let us treat one another accordingly.

The story of Ebed-melech is the story of a man who lent a helping hand out of obedience to God and out of brotherly love. The role he had to play in God's scheme of things was just as crucial as Jeremiah's, even though he is not as well known. More importantly, his example is one we need to note and follow. For there are still Jeremiahs in the well, and we need to get them out. "Pastor, what do you mean that there are Jeremiahs in the well and we need to get them out?" I'll tell you what I mean:

I mean that there are infants and children trapped in the well of hunger and poverty simply because they were born black in America; we need to get them out.

I mean that there are youth trapped in the well of poor education and miseducation simply because they were born black in America; we need to get them out.

I mean that there are young men and young women trapped in the well of unemployment and lack of opportunity simply because they were born black in America; we need to get them out.

I mean that there are elderly men and women trapped in the well of no health care and with access denied to medical facilities simply because they were born black in America; we need to get them out.

We can get them out with God's help, even if it means one child at a time, one person at a time, one well at a time. Yes, we can get them out. If only we take that first step, then God will do the rest.

No doubt about it. God is able to make a way where there was no way before,

God is able to make obstacles disappear.

God is able to rebuild broken-down bridges.

God is able to restore the washed-out roads.

God is able to open locked doors.

God is able to neutralize hidden dangers.

God is able to stem the floods.

God is able to calm the storm.

God is able to rescue stranded Jeremiahs.

We can take a lesson from Ebed-melech and make ourselves available for service. Regardless of the risk, let us lend the helping hand to one another. God stands ready to help us all.

# Bibliography

Asante, Molefe Kete, *Afrocentricity:* Trenton: Africa World Press, 1989.

ben-Jochannan, Yosef A. A. *The African Origins of the Major "Western Religions,"* Baltimore: Black Classic Press, 1991.

Bernal, Martin. *Black Athena: The Afroasiatic Roots of Classical Civilization.* Vol. 1, *The Fabrication of Ancient Greece.* New Brunswick: Rutgers University Press, 1987. Vol. 2, *The Archaeological and Documentary Evidence.* New Brunswick: Rutgers University Press, 1991.

Diop, Cheikh Anta. *The African Origin of Civilization: Myth or Reality?* Translated by Mercer Cook. Westport, Conn.: Lawrence Hill and Co., 1974.

Eisler, Robert. *The Messiah Jesus and John the Baptist according to Flavius Josephus' Recently Rediscovered "Capture of Jerusalem" and Other Jewish and Christian Sources.* Translated by Alexander Haggarty Krappe. London: Methuen, 1931.

Felder, Cain Hope. *Troubling Biblical Waters: Race, Class, and Family.* Maryknoll, N.Y.: Orbis Books, 1989.

———, ed. *Stony the Road We Trod: African American Biblical Interpretation.* Minneapolis: Fortress Press, 1991.

Hyman, Mark. *Blacks Who Died for Jesus: A History Book.* Nashville: Winston-Derek Publishers, 1988.

Jackson, John G. *Introduction to African Civilizations.* Secaucus, N.J.: Citadel Press, 1970.

James, George G. M. *Stolen Legacy: Greek Philosophy Is Stolen Egyptian Philosophy.* Newport News, Va.: United Brothers Communications System, 1989.

Johnson, John L., *The Black Biblical Heritage: Four Thousand Years of Black Biblical History* (Nashville: Winston-Derek Publishers, 1991).

McCray, Walter Arthur. *The Black Presence in the Bible and the Table of Nations, Genesis 10:1-32, with Emphasis on the Hamitic Genealogical Line from a Black Perspective.* Chicago: Black Light Fellowship, 1990.

———. *The Black Presence in the Bible: Discovering the Black and African Identity of Biblical Persons and Nations.* Chicago: Black Light Fellowship, 1990, pp. 125–129.

Mbiti, John S. *African Religions and Philosophy.* Garden City, N.Y.: Doubleday and Co., 1970.

Moore, Robert B. *Racism in the English Language: A Lesson Plan and Study Essay.* New York: Council on Interracial Books for Children, 1985.

Mosley, William. *What Color Was Jesus?* Chicago: African-American Images, 1987.

Rogers, J. A. *Nature Knows No Color-Line: Research into the Negro Ancestry in the White Race.* St. Petersburg: Helga M. Rogers, 1952; reprint 1980.

Rogers, J. A. *Sex and Race: Negro-Caucasian Mixing in All Ages and All Lands.* Vol. 1, *The Old World.* 1952. Reprint. St. Petersburg: Helga M. Rogers, 1968. Vol. 2, *A History of White, Negro, and Indian Miscegenation in the Two Americas.* 1942. Reprint. St. Petersburg, Helga M. Rogers, 1971. Vol. 3, *Why White and Black Mix in Spite of Opposition.* 1944. Reprint. St. Petersburg, Helga M. Rogers, 1972.

———. *World's Great Men of Color.* Vol. 1. Edited by John Henrik Clarke. New York: Collier Books-Macmillan Publishing Co., 1972.

Snowden, F. M., Jr. *Blacks in Antiquity: Ethiopians in the Greco-Roman Experience.* Cambridge: The Belnap Press of the Harvard University Press, 1970.

———. "Early Christianity and Blacks." In *The Interpreter's Dictionary of the Bible: Supplementary Volume.* Nashville: Abingdon Press, 1976.

Williams, Chancellor. *The Destruction of Black Civilization: Great Issues of a Race from 4500 B.C. to 2000 A.D.* Chicago: Third World Press, 1990.

# Index of Ancient Sources

## OLD TESTAMENT

# NEW TESTAMENT

# EXTRABIBLICAL LITERATURE

# Index of
# Subjects and Names